Marxism and Other Western Fallacies

MARXISM
AND OTHER WESTERN FALLACIES

An Islamic Critique

Ali Shari'ati

Translated by R. Campbell

Contemporary Islamic Thought
Persian Series
Hamid Algar, Editor

 MIZAN PRESS, Berkeley

Library of Congress Cataloging in Publication Data
Shari'ati, 'Ali.
    Marxism and other Western fallacies.

    (Contemporary Islamic thought: Persian series)
    Based on the author's Insan, Islam va maktabha-yi
Magrib' zamin.
    1. Islam—20th century. I. Title. II. Series.
BP163.S516   297'.2   79-29729
ISBN 0-933782-06-3 hard cover
ISBN 0-933782-05-5 paperback

Manufactured in the United States of America

Contents

Preface

THIS IS A BOOK that speaks for itself too eloquently to need a lengthy and laudatory introduction. The appreciation of its intrinsic interest may, however, be enhanced by an awareness of the political and intellectual context in which it was produced—that of Islamic Iran moving inexorably forward to the heroic destruction of one of the most hideous tyrannies of modern times and the immense task of creating a new state, society, economy, and culture.

Among the architects of this movement, the most important is indisputably Imam Khomeini himself, who in rare, almost unique fashion has come not only to exercise political and religious leadership, but also to be the symbol of Iranian nationhood and, beyond that, a precious exemplar of the human ideal of Islam. But other than Imam Khomeini, no one has had a more penetrating influence than the writer of this work, the late Ali Shari'ati. We will not repeat here the detailed and analytical biography of Shari'ati that has been published elsewhere,[1] but instead draw attention to the amplitude and depth of his posthumous influence on the Iranian revolution.

In all the diverse speeches, lectures and writings of Shari'ati, there is barely a single reference to the political, economic and other miseries of Pahlavi Iran, and yet it is necessary now to designate him as the chief ideologue of the Iranian Islamic

---

[1] See the bibliographical introduction by Gholam Abbas Tavassoli to *On the Sociology of Islam: Lectures by Ali Shari'ati*, trans. Hamid Algar (Berkeley: Mizan Press, 1979), pp. 11-38.

revolution. His lectures at the Husayniya-yi Irshad[2] in Tehran and in other forums around Iran (the texts of which were generally recorded, transcribed, and disseminated throughout the country) awakened new interest and confidence in Islam, not merely as a private form of worship, but as a total world-view (*jahanbini*, one of his favorite terms), fully autonomous, superior to the creeds and ideologies of past and present, and bearing in its heart a revolutionary mission. A large number of the secularly educated intelligentsia who had become alienated from Islam—and thereby from their society and the masses of the Iranian nation—were drawn again to Islam as the pivotal point of both personal existence and national destiny by the eloquence, range, and originality of Shari'ati's thought. He had a style unique among modern Muslim thinkers. He had mastered (in every sense of the word) the intellectual legacy and actuality of the West, and, eschewing apologetics, superficial modernism, and the mechanical coupling of "the best of both worlds," he was able to set against it a coherent, fresh, and powerful vision of the spiritual and philosophical essence of Islam, a vision that millions of Iranians found inspiring and convincing. Further, Shari'ati endowed the discussion of religious topics in Iran with a new tone of thought, a new style of discourse, and a whole set of new terms. This, indeed, was a revolutionary achievement.

This achievement bore fruit in the twelve months of intensified struggle, beginning in January 1978, that led to the overthrow of the Pahlavi dynasty and the birth of the Islamic Republic of Iran. As the mosques of Iran became the ideological and organizational centers of the revolution, echoes from the work and ideas of Ali Shari'ati could be heard in many of the sermons and addresses that inspired the Iranian Muslim people to seek martyrdom. Memorable sentences from his writings served as ready-made revolutionary slogans, without

---

[2] Husayniya-yi Irshad: an institution of religious discussion and instruction where, beginning in 1968, Shari'ati delivered most of his important lectures to overflow crowds. Closed by the Shah's regime in 1973, it was reopened immediately after the Islamic revolution in February 1979.

need for any elaboration or commentary, and they were inscribed on banners carried in all of the great demonstrations of the Iranian revolution: "The martyr is the heart of history!" "Every day is Ashura; every place is Karbala!" Most importantly, many of those who with their blood bought the foundation of the Islamic Republic in this world, and Paradise in the hereafter, were, directly or indirectly, the pupils of Shari'ati.

On April 23, 1979, a terrorist group by the name of Forqan assassinated General Muhammad Vali Qarani, first chief of staff of the Iranian armed forces after the revolution. This was followed on May 1 by the murder of Ayatullah Murtaza Mutahhari, a close associate of Imam Khomeini, and three weeks later by an attempt on the life of Ayatullah Hashimi Rafsinjani; Forqan also claimed responsibility for those crimes. In a communique forwarded to the Tehran newspaper *Ayandegan*—always eager to print such material, before it was closed down by the revolutionary prosecutor—the anonymous hands of Forqan wrote that they were in the service of the thought of Shari'ati and attempting to realize his alleged vision of an Islam without *akhunds*, i.e., institutionalized religious leadership.

It is highly probable that Forqan is ultimately under the command of persons owing their allegiance to the former regime, and possibly, also, to the American patrons of that discredited tyranny. Certainly American officialdom has begun showing a remarkable interest in the work of Shari'ati. For example, in January, the State Department began making inquiries concerning his thought and influence, and three months later, attempts were made to recruit someone to brief Cutler, then ambassador-designate to Iran, on the same subject. Once the activities of Forqan are considered in the context of continual imperialist activity to destabilize the Islamic Republic of Iran, they appear as a tactic designed to create a dichotomy in the Islamic movement: on the one side, the posthumous following of Shari'ati, "anti-clerical" in its attitudes, and opposing them, those loyal to the religious leadership, above all Imam Khomeini.

Given this probable counterrevolutionary direction of the activities of Forqan, it may be conceded that some of the followers of the movement—those entrusted with the business of killing—genuinely believe in the necessity for eradicating the *ulama*. All too numerous in Iran are young people whose acquaintance with Islam is recent and superficial, and for whom Islam means, above all, a permanent and unbridled revolutionary fervor. As the late Ayatullah Mutahhari pointed out, hypocrites always need fools to carry out their plans, and it is likely that Forqan is indeed an alliance of scheming hypocrites and gullible fools. The most effective way to recruit the fools, it appears, has been to invoke Shari'ati as the alleged ideologue of anti-clerical Islam.

Because certain pseudo-academic authorities have attempted to legitimize this claim of Forqan to the legacy of Shari'ati[3], we would like to clarify here the attitudes that Shari'ati did in fact hold toward the *ulama*, the traditional leaders. It is obvious that he was not of their number, and that his ideas and expression bore a "modern" stamp that did not always correspond to their taste. His works are replete with references to Western thought and history, and even though

---

[3] See, for example, Mangol Bayat, "Iran's Real Revolutionary Leader," *Christian Science Monitor*, May 24, 1979. This article is replete with distortions and misconceptions. Bayat claims, *inter alia*, that Shari'ati "was to a large extent influenced by Marxist social ideas." (Readers of the present work can easily assess the accuracy of that statement!) She further maintains that Shari'ati dismissed Qum, the major center of Islamic learning, as "an inadequate center of religion in Iran"—an assessment nowhere to be found in his works—and claims that the late Mutahhari "personified all that Shari'ati and his followers stood and fought against." This statement overlooks, among other things, the fact that Shari'ati collaborated with Ayatullah Mutahhari at the Husayniya-yi Irshad and on a number of occasions makes respectful reference to him in his works (e.g., *Husayn Vares-i Adam* ["Husayn, the Heir of Adam"] [Tehran: n.d.], notes, p. 19). How, then, could there have been such a diametrical opposition between the two men? Bayatt's claim is a gratuitous insult to the memory of both men, who struggled for the sake of the same ideal and were cut down by the same forces, forces that have unceasingly conspired against the freedom and dignity of the Iranian people.

these references are for the most part negative, they must have had a jarring effect on an extremely traditionalist audience. Shari'ati discerns, moreover, as a perpetual and universal sociological phenomenon, the existence of an "official" clergy, allied with the oppressive state and the holders of wealth, as a major component in the system of injustice. Such a clergy may exist even in an Islamic and Shi'i setting, and Shari'ati designated the celebrated Baqir Majlisi (d. 1699) as a representative of that class, the function of which is to destroy rather than to serve religion.

None of this means, however, that Shari'ati rejected the institution of religious leadership. Non-traditional is different from anti-traditional, and criticism of certain religious leaders of the past by no means implies a partial, or, still less, a total, repudiation of those of the present. Shari'ati clarified his attitude to the ulama by denying them "official" (rasmi) standing on the one hand, and by regarding them as fulfilling an essential need (zarurat) on the other. That is, donning the garb of the religious scholar confers no privilege or special status, and is in no way akin to being ordained a Christian priest. There is a real and practical need for the cultivation of expertise in religious knowledge, and herein lies the function undertaken by the ulama on behalf of the community. In addressing themselves to this task, the ulama are not merely legitimate, they are indispensable.[4]

It should further be noted that many of the particular criticisms of the social and political shortcomings of the ulama made by Shari'ati have also been raised with some insistence by Imam Khomeini himself. In the lectures he gave at Najaf in 1969, Khomeini repeatedly castigated those religious scholars who confined their attention to the minor details of ritual purity for betraying the dignity and true mission of their class.[5] Despite differences of tone and emphasis, both Shari'ati and Imam Khomeini have contributed to the revival

[4] Ali Shari'ati, "Shi'a," *Majmu'a-yi Asar* ("Collected Works") (Tehran: 1357/1958), VII, p. 182.

[5] Ayatullah Ruhullah Khomeini, *Hukumat-i Islami* (Najaf: 1391/1971), pp. 11, 24-25.

of religious thought and activism in Iran, and their influences have been exercised in largely complementary fashion. Anyone only slightly acquainted with the Iranian revolution knows that countless Iranians regard themselves simultaneously as the followers of Imam Khomeini and as the disciples of the late Ali Shari'ati, and this entails neither divided loyalties nor mental contortions. Those who hope to exploit the ignorance and excessive fervor of a minority of young Iranians in order to create warring camps in the Islamic revolution and thereby to destroy it are liable to be disappointed.

The Iranian revolution has been, among other things, an implicit repudiation of Marxism as a revolutionary ideology and as a doctrine relevant to the problems of Iranian society or valid for humanity at large. In the West much was heard, during the course of the Iranian revolution, about "an unnatural alliance between Marxists and Muslims," which was bound to end with the Marxists' swallowing up the Muslims after the overthrow of the Shah. (By contrast, few observers in the West paid any attention to the grotesque array of powers, great and small, that supported and applauded the Shah.) Events since the revolution, as well as the actual course of the revolution itself, have proven, however, how weak and ineffective the Iranian left really is. This situation is partly the result of the errors and even crimes committed over the years by various Marxist groups in Iran. But it is also the result of an ideological debate and confrontation that was carried on both in Iran and in the Iranian revolutionary diaspora during the last decade or so of the Pahlavi dictatorship. The opposition of Muslim and Marxist is by no means over, either in Iran or elsewhere; but the Iranian revolution certainly shows the debate to be going in favor of the Muslims. A number of important and influential refutations of Marxism have helped to achieve this result. We should mention *Darsha'i dar barayi Marksism* ("Lessons on Marxism") by Jalal ud-Din Farisi, *Naqdi va daramadi bar tazadd-i dialektiki* ("A Critical Introduction to the Theory of Dialectic Contradiction") by Abd ul-Karim Sarush, and the various writings by Ali Shari'ati, especially the present collection.[6]

What distinguishes all of these books (particularly those of Shari'ati), and sets them apart from most critiques of Marxism attempted elsewhere in the Islamic world, are (1) an intimate knowledge of Marxism and its philosophical foundations and (2) the attempt to point out logical contradictions within Marxism, instead of adducing scriptural arguments to underline the well-known differences between Islam and Marxism. Shari'ati is aided in his task of refutation by a thorough acquaintance with the predecessors of Marxism in European thought and the circumstances of intellectual history that have left an indelible Western stamp on the doctrine, despite its having been exported to the Third World as a supposed means for combating the West. His critique of Marxism is situated, moreover, in the context of a coherent vision and statement of Islam as ideology; it is plain that his strictures on Marxism are not motivated by mere negative animus. The combination of these factors permits an analysis and a refutation that are serene and self-assured as well as radical and uncompromising.

The bulk of the present work consists of a series of privately given lectures, the text of which was published under a succession of different circumstances. After the release of Ali Shari'ati from his second imprisonment in 1977, the text was serialized in the Tehran daily newspaper *Kayhan*, from February 15 to March 15, 1977, under the title, "Man, Marxism and Islam." This printing took place without the consent of Shari'ati, and was intended by the Shah's regime to discredit him by planting the suggestion that he had decided to collaborate, and that this indeed was the reason for his release from prison. Shari'ati protested, and even attempted to take legal action against the editors of *Kayhan*, but to no avail. The text was

---

[6] Also to be mentioned in this context are two influential works in Arabic by Ayatullah Muhammad Baqir as-Sadr, a *mujtahid* resident in Najaf and a long-standing acquaintance of Imam Khomeini—*Falsafatuna* ("Our Philosophy") (2nd ed. Beirut: 1390/1969) and *Iqtisaduna* ("Our Economy") (new ed. Beirut: 1398/1977), both of which contain important sections in refutation of Marxism.

then reprinted abroad in book form under the title *Man, Islam and Western Schools of Thought*. This text in turn became the basis for numerous copies circulated during the year of revolution, and it is also the basis for this translation. Our title for the series, "Marxism and Other Western Fallacies," is the coinage of the editor.

The second and briefer text contained in this volume, "Mysticism, Equality, and Freedom," was published for the first time in 1978 in the second volume of Shari'ati's collected works (pp. 61-90). Since it discusses some of the same major themes as the first text, although with somewhat different emphases, it seemed useful to include it here as a kind of supplement. It was transcribed from a tape-recording of one of Shari'ati's numerous lectures and, because its publication was posthumous, could not be revised by him. His father, however, Mohammad Taqi Shari'ati, did have the opportunity to read over the manuscript before that printing and thought it appropriate to add, in the form of footnotes, a few paragraphs of explanatory matter. In the present edition, his name appears in parentheses after these notes.

Both texts included in this volume are faithful and complete renderings of the original. The few liberties taken by the translator have been for the purposes of excising the repetitions and tightening the loose syntactic structure that almost inevitably characterizes the style of an extemporaneous lecture.

The numerous quotations from Marx and other writers that occur in the texts are often approximate paraphrases made by Shari'ati in the course of his lecturing. No attempt has been made, therefore, to identify their precise sources.

I would like to express my thanks to Heidi Bendorf for her assistance in reading and editing the manuscript.

Hamid Algar

Berkeley
Zihijja 1400/November 1979

MARXISM AND OTHER WESTERN FALLACIES

On Humanism

IT IS VIRTUALLY IMPOSSIBLE to agree upon a precise and logical definition of what is human, since such a definition will vary according to the scientific perspective, philosophical school, or religious belief under consideration.

Nor has science been able to remove the mystery from this microcosm. As Alexis Carrel said, "To the same extent that man has been occupied with the external world and has achieved progress there, he has become distanced from himself and has forgotten his own reality." It is no accident that Carrel, founder of *la Fondation francaise pour l'etude des problemes humains* and one of the most outstanding figures of our age, spoke of man as "the unknown." Nevertheless, one cannot abandon the attempt to achieve knowledge of man, to form an accurate conception of his essence and substantive reality, since, to begin with, knowledge of the human means knowledge of ourselves, and without it we are enveloped in such a darkness of self-ignorance that the shining lamp of science, awareness, is incapable of guiding us anywhere.

This deficiency amounts to a calamity that, despite man's stunning successes in the world of science, has deprived him of a correct understanding of the meaning of life, of the significance of his own existence. According to Dewey, it shows that he is weaker and more ignorant in self-governance than ancient man.

Now, knowledge of this unknown, humanity, is more urgently needed than any other kind of knowledge. This is truly vital information! It is no exaggeration to say that the basic reason all contemporary scientific, social, and ideological attempts to truly liberate mankind, or even impart to it a feeling of well-being, have failed is precisely this: the locus of all these attempts and relative successes—which is the human being—has remained unknown, or been forgotten, in one way or another.

It is altogether in vain that some of our foremost engineers and architects, on the basis of highly sophisticated technical principles, speak of the best and most convenient home before understanding the character of the family that must live in that home: what personality types it embraces, what attitudes and goals its members hold, what their basic needs are.

Stunning advances have been made by the modern educational system, which include the latest scientific discoveries in the field of psychology and the great technological possibilities before it. Despite these, however, not only have there been no brilliant successes (other than the mobilization of a new generation to pursue scientific and technical learning and intellectual growth), but also, from numerous standpoints, even by comparison with the instructional systems and disciplines of the past, the result has been a sterility.

And so it is that modern man, more than any of his predecessors, can construct man, but knows less than any of them what it is he is constructing. As for his life, he can also live any sort of life he pleases, but he does not know *how* because he does not know *why*. These are the basic questions that no one can find answers for in the capitalist societies, and no one has the courage to frame in the communist societies.

It is here that we may say why these new ideologies that try so hard to replace the ancient religions fall short of answering basic human needs, and why, in the end, they either lead people to a sense of futility, or draw them into bondage. In addition, the philosophy of human life has no place in either of the two established worlds of Western liberalism and Eastern communism, for in both, what has been sacrificed is the free growth of the essential nature of man. Before we come to draw this conclusion, however, we must know the meaning of the essential nature of man; then we may discuss its free growth, its alteration, and its degradation.

Thus we return to the need for a definition of the substance and essential reality of the human, because the human is the criterion for the worth or uselessness of every school and every way of life.

DESPITE ALL THE AMBIGUITY that exists for science about the meaning of human existence, and despite the fact that each philosophical school and each religion explains it in a different way, we may agree as to the most essential shared bases upon which the major schools of scientific, religious, and social thought mount their view of man.

The aggregate of these generally accepted assumptions may be designated "humanism," referring to the school that proclaims its essential goal to be the liberation and perfection of man, whom it considers a primary being, and the principles of which are based on response to those basic needs that form the specificity of man.

Today, we face four intellectual currents that claim, despite their mutually contradictory natures, to represent this humanism: (1) Western liberalism, (2) Marxism, (3) existentialism, and (4) religion.

Western liberalism perceives itself as the principal heir of the philosophy and culture of historical liberalism, envisioned as a continuous flow of culture and thought issuing from ancient Greece and reaching its relative perfection in present-day Europe. Western humanism rests firmly on the foundation of that mythological perspective unique to ancient Greece, where between heaven and earth (the world of the gods and the world of men), competitiveness, opposition, and even a sort of jealousy obtain, and the gods are anti-human forces, whose every inclination and striving is to rule tyrannically over humanity and discourage it from attaining self-awareness, independence, freedom, and sovereignty over nature. Any human who sets foot upon any of these paths has perpetrated a great sin—has risen in rebellion against the gods—and is condemned to the most severe tortures and punishments in the afterlife. Humanity, we may say, is constantly seeking its liberation from this captivity. It strives to attain independence through the acquisition of divine powers, in order to free its destiny from the grasp of the gods' omnipotence and bring it within reach of its own free will and choice.

Of course, such a bond of enmity between men and gods was altogether natural and logical to the Greek myths—from a certain point of view, proper and even progressive, since the gods in these myths constitute archetypes and expressions of natural forces such as seas, rivers, earth, rain, beauty, physical strength, economic abundance, and seasons of the year, as well as storms, earthquakes, illnesses, drought, and so on. Thus, the war between the gods and men is in reality the latter's war against dominance by the physical forces that rule over human life, will, and fate; through its ever-increasing power and awareness, humanity strives to free itself from the rule of those forces and become its own ruler. It struggles to triumph over nature, the greatest established power—that is, to supplant Zeus, who symbolizes the rule of nature over mankind.

The greatest, most astounding sophistry that the modern humanists—from Diderot and Voltaire to Feuerbach and Marx—have committed is this: they have equated the mythical world of ancient Greece, which remains within the bounds of material nature, with the spiritual and sacred world of the great ancient religions. They have compared and even bracketed together humanity's relation to Zeus and its relation to Ahuramazda, Rama, the Tao, the Messiah, and Allah, whereas these two sets of relations are in truth antithetical.

In the former world, Prometheus, who gave the "divine fire" to mankind, first robs the gods of the fire as they sleep and brings it secretly to earth, then is sentenced for this sin to suffer tortures at the hands of the gods. In the world of the last of these, God's highest-ranking angel, Iblis, becomes accursed of God because, unlike the rest of the angels, he refuses to prostrate himself at the feet of Adam, as God has ordered. Furthermore, the "divine fire," in the form of the heavenly light of wisdom, of revelation, is entrusted by God to His prophets so that it might be brought to humanity and, with the aspirations that accompany it, hope and fear of God, summon Adam's progeny from realms of darkness to this light.

We see that in this case, in contrast to Zeus, God wishes humanity to be free of the great yoke of slavery to nature; He proclaims its road to deliverance to be the pursuit of that same Promethean light. We must conclude that in the world-view of the great religions, God summons humanity to victory over Zeus and proclaims, "All the angels have prostrated themselves at the feet of Adam, and land and sea have been made tame for you."

Thus, in the mythic world-view of ancient Greece, it is natural and logical that a humanism should develop in opposition to rule by, and worship of, the gods—the archetypes of nature—and that there should exist an opposition between humanism and theism (or, in this instance, polytheism).

On this basis, Greek humanism, through denial of the gods, disbelief in their rule, and severance of the bond between man and heaven, struggled to arrive at an anthropocentric universe—to make man the touchstone of truth and falsity, to take the human form as the criterion of beauty, and to assign importance to the components of life that enhance human power and pleasure.

Inasmuch as this anthropocentricity took the form of opposition to the heavenly, it became earthly and tended toward materialism. Thus humanism in the Western perspective— from ancient Greece to present-day Europe—has been drawn into materialism, and it has undergone a similar fate in the liberalism of the encyclopedists, in Western bourgeois culture, and in Marxism.

Also inducing humanism in the West to take the form of something all the more antithetical to theism was the Catholicism of the Middle Ages, which set Christianity (regarded as religion *per se*) at odds with humanity: it maintained the same opposition between heaven and earth that had obtained in ancient Greece and Rome; and, with its Greek-style exegeses of original sin and man's expulsion from Paradise, it represented man as helplessly condemned because of divine displeasure to an inferior world, and declared him to be an abject, reprehensible, and weak sinner. It excepted only that class of human society known as the clergy, the bearers of the spirit, and held that the only means of salvation for the rest of the people lay in following them without why or wherefore, in blind imitation, and through membership in the institution by means of which the officially recognized manifestations of God on earth were administered.

This sort of thinking pitted theism against humanism. So the road to the realization of divine rule necessarily led past the altar on which humanism was sacrificed, thus disappearing in the Middle Ages. In science and culture, in life and morals, even in the art and aesthetics of the Middle Ages, confidence ceases to be reposed in humanity. All of the artistic and aesthetic manifestations of the Middle Ages are depictions of the supernatural and superhuman: the Holy Spirit, the Savior, the angels, various miracles. If the human figure appears, it is only in the persons of the apostles and saints, and even then, their human forms are enshrouded head to toe in long, loose-fitting garments and, generally speaking, their faces are veiled or obscured by a halo of celestial light.

Literature? The transmission of these tales.

Art? The depiction of these fables.

Science? The validation of these conceptions.

Morals? The suppression of all natural desires in order to atone for original sin.

Life in this world? It must be sacrificed in order to achieve life in the next.

We see everywhere in medieval Catholicism that it is by the negation of genuinely human traits that man is to reach God; that is to say, he is to become the object of God's good pleasure. How closely this Christian God resembles Zeus! Thus if we may speak of the post-Renaissance humanism of modern Europe as a continuation of the humanism of ancient Greece, we may speak equally well of a "celestialism" in medieval Christianty as being a continuation of the celestialism of the Greek myths. In the West, whether during the Middle Ages or modern times, everyone draws from the well-spring of Greece; the history of Western culture is the persistence of these two contrasting currents that issue from the same spring, whether we refer to religion or science.

Now the situation becomes clearer. Both these divergent streams of today have their fountainhead in Greek humanism. Bourgeois liberalism and Marxism alike share, in theory and in practice, this human materialism; Voltaire and Marx both closed their eyes to the spiritual dimensions of the human essence. Bourgeois liberal society and organized communist society ultimately converge in a single view of humanity, human life, and human society. The bourgeois tendencies of the advanced communist societies—which can no longer be simply dismissed—are no accident, no aberration, no revisionist deviation, because everything culminates in man, and it is only natural that those philosophies that have a similar conception of man, no matter what their starting point, should finally enter upon the same road and have the same final destination.

At any rate, Western bourgeois liberalism and Marxism both boast of their humanism. The former claims, by leaving individuals free to think and to pursue scientific research, intellectual encounter, and economic production, to lead to a blossoming of human talents. The latter claims to reach the same goal through the denial of those freedoms, through their confinement under a dictatorial leadership that manages society as a single organization, on the basis of a single ideology that imparts to peoples a monotonous uniformity. The real philosophy of man and life, however, is the same that lies dormant within the liberal bourgeois philosophy: the extension of the life of the bourgeoisie to all members of society.

So it is perhaps not in jest that it has been said: "Is not Marxism more bourgeois than the bourgeoisie?"

Well, it is jesting, which, from the point of view of humanism, is an actual fact.

Just as the bourgeois liberalism of the West sees itself as the heir to historical humanistic culture, and Marxism presents itself as a path for the realization of humanism, of the whole man, so existentialism is a humanism, and of course a more rightful claimant to humanism than its two predecessors.

There is still a fourth great intellectual current, older and more deeply rooted than all three of these, and that is the religious world-view. Given that each religion proclaims its mission to be the guidance of humanity to its ultimate salvation, each necessarily has its own specific anthropology, in that one may not speak of human salvation until the meaning of the human has been clarified. Thus, all religions begin with a philosophy of creation, and of human creation.

Accordingly, using these four varied intellectual streams current in today's world, which have conceived of humanity as a principle or a principial species and base thereon their claims for applicability, we may attempt a definition of man that will serve as a single point of departure to the matters at issue.

THE RADICALISTS—who were among the most outstanding exponents and intellectuals of the "new humanism" of eighteenth- and early nineteenth-century Europe—proclaimed in a manifesto that they published in 1800: "Set aside God as the basis of morals and replace Him with Conscience." They held that man is a being that in and of himself possesses a moral conscience, which in their view springs from his original and essential character, and which his human nature requires.[1] This reliance upon human nature, as well as upon moral conscience, forms the fundamental basis of the Western atheistic humanism of the present age.

With the advent of the age of scientific analysis, and in particular the development of sociology (which has disarmed

---

[1] This despite the fact that this philosophy, as an educational system, had such unfortunate consequences that it was officially discontinued and disappeared from the schools. As Isoulet has said, "This method caused a moral turpitude to appear in France; it threatened to ruin all the efforts made since the time of Socrates to raise God above the ethical infrastructure."

psychology and put it to flight), human nature as an underlying principle became subject to, first, doubt, and then, outright denial. At that point, moral conscience, instead of supposedly springing from the depths of this nature, was transformed into a social conscience rooted in the necessarily mutable aspect of the human social environment and so, likewise mutable. Thus, morals as a set of sacred and transcendental values fell victim to upheaval and were nearly eliminated.

Nonetheless, the new humanism—upon which Western bourgeois liberalism as a system is based—regards humanity as possessing eternal moral virtues and noble, supramaterial values for which man is the essential focus. It is at this point that it places its reliance upon man *in and of himself*, as against nature or the supernatural.

This humanism arrogates human morals as a whole from religion, but, while denying their religious rationale, it proclaims the possibility of spiritual development and growth in adherence to the moral virtues without belief in God.

On this matter, there are two differing aspects of Marxism; one has Marx opposed to the capitalist order of his time and attacking it forcefully, and the other has him go on to set forth a properly communist social order. In the latter, the "affirmative" aspect of Marxism, it seems that Marx allowed his marvelous sensitivity to human moral values to be overshadowed by his revolutionary enthusiasm for the politics and economics of communism, and thus allows himself to be transformed into just another political leader, hungry for power and enamored of political triumph.

However, in his "critical" phase—the aspect of Marx that is more intriguing and has attracted the hearts and minds of so many of those oppressed by capitalism—he shows this sensitivity clearly when he attacks the system as one that "degrades the higher values of humanity." Assuming a mystical tone, he speaks of humanity as zealous, self-aware, truthful, proud, free, knowing, endowed with moral virtues—as having become alienated from itself in the "heartless, oppressive, unfeeling" system of mechanism, and in the "exploitation, moral corruption, and egotism" of capitalism. He cries out, "Work is essential to humanity; capitalism regards it as a material product and assigns a monetary value to it, so the worker is made a slave to his stomach."

When he speaks of the principle of production, however, the value of the tools of production, the principle of economic abundance, and, in particular, the creation of an economic plan for all society under socialism, this mystical tone changes to a materialistic tone.

In the negative [critical] aspect of Marxism, the glorification of humanity reaches a pitch that has prompted such scholars as Aron, Duverger, and even Henri Lefebvre—in jest or seriously—to speak of a "mystical humanism" in Marx's critical and philosophical works.

Existentialism, with prodigious philosophizing, speaks of humanity as a separately spun cord loose in the world, a being having no determinative character or quality owed to God or nature, but capable of choice, and thus constructing and creating its own reality.

In the great Eastern religions, humanity has a unique relationship with the God of the world. In the religion of Zoroaster mankind is the companion of Ahuramazda and even allies itself with him in the great battle of creation, for the sake of victory of the good over Angra Mainyu and his hosts. In the mystical religions based upon the Unity of Existence—and at the heart of them all, Hinduism—God, mankind, and love are all seen as engaged in a sort of scheme to re-create the world of existence. Man and God in this religion are so intermingled as to be essentially inseparable, as they likewise appear in the works of our great Sufis.

In Islam, although the interval stretching from man to God extends to infinity, that from God to man is altogether eliminated. Man is presented as the sole being within creation having the divine spirit, bearing the responsibility of the divine trust, and finding incumbent upon it the assumption of divine qualities.

The most basic of the specifically human qualities, by the general consent of humanists, may now be delineated:

1. Man is a primary being. That is, among all natural and supernatural beings, man has an independent self and a noble essence.

2. Man is an independent volition. This is his most extraordinary and inexplicable power: volition in the sense that humanity has entered into that chain of causation upon which the world of nature, history, and society are completely dependent as a primary and independent cause, and continues to intervene in and act upon this deterministic series.

Freedom and choice, his two existential determinations, have imparted to him a godlike quality.

3. Man is an aware being. This is his most outstanding quality: awareness in the sense that, through the wonderful and miraculous power of reflection, he comprehends the actualities of the external world, discovers the secrets hidden to these senses, and is able to analyze each reality and each event. He does not remain on the surface of sensibles and effects, but discerns what is beyond the sensible, and induces the cause from the effect. In this way, he both transcends the limits of his senses and extends his temporal ties into the past and the future, into times in which he has no objective presence; he acquires a correct, broad, and profound grasp of his own environment.

In the words of Pascal, "Man is nothing more than a delicate reed. A humble drop is sufficient to annihilate him, but even if all the world undertakes his perdition, he is nonetheless more noble than all the world: the world is unaware that it is annihilating man, but man knows he is being annihilated." That is to say, awareness is a nobler substance than existence.

4. Man is a self-conscious being. This means he is the only living being possessing knowledge of his own presence. He is able to study himself and thus to analyze, know, evaluate, and consequently change himself—as a being independent of himself. Toynbee, that great contemporary philosopher of history, says, "Today's human civilization has arrived at the highest stage of its historical perfection, in that it is only today's civilization that knows itself to be in decline"!

5. Man is a creative being. This creative aspect of his behavior sets him altogether apart from nature, and places him beside God; it puts him in possession of a quasi-miraculous power that enables him to transcend the natural parameters

of his own existence, grants him a limitless existential expansion and breadth, and places him in a position to enjoy what nature has not given him.

It also gives him this power in relation to the heart of nature: what he wishes for that does not exist in nature he creates. Thus, it was by this creative power of his that, in the first stage of his development, he produced tools, and in the second, the arts.

6. Man is an idealistic being, a worshipper of the ideal. By this is meant that he is never content with what is but strives to transform it into what ought to be. That is why he is constantly engaged in re-creating; and why he demonstrates that he is the only being not the product of but rather the producer of his environment, or to put it simply, why he is constantly engaged in making reality conform to his idea. Thus, not only is he in a state of constant movement, movement toward perfection, but, in contrast with other living beings, he determines the course of his own evolution and can exercise foresight in relation to it.

Idealism is the major factor in human movement and evolution; it leaves no room for staying contentedly within the fixed confines of existing reality (of nature or of ways of life). It is this force that constantly compels man to reflect, discover, research, realize, invent, and create, in the physical and the spiritual realm.

Crafts, art, literary pursuits, and all the riches of human culture are manifestations of the idealistic spirit of this being that never resigns itself to the situation that the world has provided for it.

7. Man is a moral being. It is here that the very significant question of value arises. Value consists of the link that exists between man and any phenomenon, behavior, act, or condition where a motive higher than that of utility is at issue; it might be called a sacred tie, as it is bound up with reverence and worship to the extent that people feel it justifiable to devote or sacrifice their very lives to this tie. Moreover, this is likewise worth considering: there is no question of a natural, rational, or scientific justification here; and also, this

sentiment, as the most sublime existential manifestation of the human species, is acknowledged in all religions and cultures throughout history as constituting the greatest of resources, the grandest of glories, the most precious of emotions, the most miraculous of events.

From those who have neglected their own material existence for the sake of art, literature, and science, to the religious martyrs, the truth-seekers, and the great heroes of each nation; from the person who, in marriage, chooses love over expediency, to the one who, for the sake of belief, country, or humanity, has closed his eyes to personal love or even to self —all are creators of human values in human life. *Value* and *utility* are two opposing terms, and what grants man, a nonmaterial being, an independence from, as well as a superiority over, all other natural beings is his high regard for value.

Values have no existence in nature, no external, material identity. Therefore, realism cannot admit the existence of values, since without humanity there would be no values. We come here to the inescapable conclusion that values emanate from man, and are therefore of the ideal or subjective order, for which reason the realists are obliged to deny them. But how can one deny the most noble existential manifestations of the human species? Of course, to do so is a difficult and likewise shameful, deadly task, but what other recourse has the realist? Unless, that is, he resorts to acknowledging man's precedence over material reality, or the precedence of mind over matter, which assertions themselves serve to deny realism.

But the realist philosophers—e.g., the materialists and naturalists who depend solely upon philosophical and scientific notions of sociology, psychology, and anthropology—do not hesitate to deny the existence of values, dismissing them as superstitions, vain suppositions, inherited habits, or social mores resulting from material forms, or as emotional states originating in the physiology of this "talking animal"! With their merciless and unfeeling pseudo-scientific analysis, the realists corrupt the essential sanctity and virtue of values and vivisect them as one cuts apart a living, delicate system into dead substance and elementary material components.

Thus, when confronted with a person who forgets himself in the pursuit of scientific discovery, or who dedicates his life to his country, or chooses ideals over self-interest, or who ascribes greater value to beauty and goodness than to personal pleasure and advantage, the realists explain his feelings just as they would explain participation in a rite of circumcision!

It is precisely here that Marxism stumbles into what is, for an ideology, a very weak position in which to be caught. For one thing, Marx is not merely a philosophical materialist, free to say along with Sartre, "Whatever you choose out of freedom, free choice, and good intentions constitutes a value and a good" (however much it might serve evil or base egoism). Marx is a social ideologist who has become political guide to the proletariat of his age and founder of a party on the "stage of action," and is thus the promulgator of a specific program; who, in contrast to Sartre, says, "These are the things you must choose," and, further: "You are held responsible for them, and in the face of these responsibilities, you must struggle and sacrifice to realize these specific ideals." That is to say, "You must offer up all your material motives, economic needs, natural wants, personal advantages, and even your life for the sake of this struggle."

There can be no doubt, therefore, that he speaks of a *set of values*—values inimical to self-interest and transcending human material existence. Thus when he speaks of the capitalist system and bourgeois psychology as appraising human existential values in terms of money, drawing humanity into moral depravity, and building a corrupt society, he bases his thought on moral values.

When he shows off the edifice of his thought, however, and discusses dialectical materialism, he struggles mightily to prove himself loyal to realism and to grant only all that fits the material and biological rationale of the natural sciences. And he follows the rest of the materialists, including the most hardened realists, in reducing human values to something with no foundation.

Marx refers repeatedly and with pride to a piece of scientific legerdemain that he has brought into play for the sake of preserving human dignity, which is this: dialectics does not conceive of man as do other forms of naturalism and materialism—that is, as a fixed material entity in a clockwork universe—but rather presents him as a being in a state of evolution, moving forward with the historical dialectics. By this stratagem, Marx transfers humanity from the realm of nature to that of history.

But man gains no nobility through this promotion. Since history, according to Marx, is "the continuation of the movement of material nature," man, in the context of history, is ultimately returned to the mechanical nature of the naturalists, to be conceived of as a material entity. Thus, all the values that Marx bestows upon him in the context of society he takes back from him with the hand of dialectical materialism. (Here Chandel's very telling remark comes to mind: "Marx the philosopher crushes all the substantive values of man under the wheels of the blind juggernaut of dialectical materialism; but Marx the politician and leader, with the most fervid and electrifying praise of these values, mobilizes people for power and victory.")

Is not Marx's reliance on these values, in whose authenticity he does not believe, simply part of his battle tactics? If so, this is a most obvious case of political chicanery.

AT ANY RATE, considering all the fundamental, uncontested assertions about man shared by the four prevailing modern intellectual currents under consideration, we may deduce the following definition: man is a primary being in the natural world, having his own unique essence, and, as a creation or as a phenomenon, is exceptional and noble. Because he possesses will, he intervenes in nature as an independent cause, possesses the power of choice, and has a hand in creating a new destiny for himself in contradistinction to his natural fate. This power brings him a commitment, a responsibility, which is meaningless unless articulated with reference to a system of values.

At the same time, man is an idealistic being who strives to transform the actual into the true—that is, "what is" into "what ought to be"—whether in the realm of nature, society, or the self. This transformation provides for movement toward perfection within him. He is also a being who demonstrates in his acts a power antithetical to nature, in that through his acts he re-creates both the world's nature and his own. Having the power of creation, he uses it to further the development of both nature's and his own existence. Accordingly, by the creation of beauty, art, and literature, he gives the material world what it lacks, and by the creation of craftworks, he provides himself with what nature has not given him.

Likewise, man is a thinking being, and with this transcendental aptitude he grows in consciousness of the world and himself, and also of his human condition in the world, in society, and in time. By means of thought, he broadens his existential scope beyond the confines of his physical existence, while his intellectual scope plunges deep below the surface of sensible phenomena and ascends to heights above the low rooftops of the material world. Where his environment comes to an end he continues, in the process of existential sublimation that is endless within him.

In sum, man bears a sacred substance, and from it flow sanctities, the worship of which is the most exalted of the supernatural and supra-logical manifestations of his existence. Taken together, these form the human values, the values that have brought into being the acts of love, worship, and sacrifice known to history that account for all of humanity's glories and spiritual resources. Human values are sacred ideas, which, although their applicability may vary, are eternal and absolute and may change only as the human species changes or disappears.

It is said that Nietzsche, the great philosopher, sacrified his life to save a draft horse. The materialist mind considers such an act not only senseless, but disastrous and deserving of condemnation, because through it a genius rather than an animal has been lost. Still, there is in this wondrous human nature an extraordinary element, which, confronted with this incident, glorifies it and gives it praise befitting something sacred. It attributes great worth to this transaction, because Nietzsche, by sacrificing himself, has created a value, a moral value, which is higher than the existential value of one body —even that of a genius.

What produces this kind of judgment and motive in man is the transcendental dimension of human existence, in denial of which materialism and dialectical materialism have denied man, and in affirming which they have denied themselves!

Modern Calamities

THE MODERN CALAMITIES that are leading to the deformation and decline of humanity may be placed under two main headings: (1) Social systems and (2) Intellectual systems.

Within the two outwardly opposed social systems that have embraced the new man, or that invite him into their embrace, what is plainly felt is the tragic way that man, a primary and supra-material essence, has been forgotten.

Both these social systems, capitalism and communism, though they differ in outward configuration, regard man as an economic animal; their differing contours reflect the issue of which of the two will provide more successfully for the needs of this animal.

Economism is the fundamental principle of the philosophy of life in Western industrial capitalist society, where, as Francis Bacon put it, "Science abandons its search for truth and turns to the search for power."

The material "needs" that are generated every day and progressively find increase (so that the scope of consumption may be enlarged in quantity, quality, and variety alike, to feed the vast engines of production as they race on in delirium) transform people into worshippers of consumption. Day by day, heavier burdens are imposed on a frenetic populace, so that modern technological prodigies, who ought to have freed mankind from servitude to manual labor and increased people's leisure time, cannot do even that much, so rapidly have artificial material needs outpaced the tremendous speed of production technology. Humanity is every day more condemned to alienation, more drowned in this mad maelstrom of compulsive speed. Not only is there no longer leisure for growth in human values, moral greatness, and spiritual aptitudes, but this being plunged headlong in working to consume, consuming to work, this diving into lunatic competition for luxuries and diversions, has caused traditional moral values to decline and disappear as well.

In communist society, we find a similar downward curve in human moral values. Many intellectuals, contemplating the political and economic contrasts between the communist and capitalist societies, account the former different from the latter from the standpoints of anthropology, philosophy of life, and humanism. But we see clearly that communist societies, although they have attained a relatively advanced stage of economic growth, closely resemble the bourgeois West with respect to social behavior, social psychology, individual outlook, and the philosophy of life and human nature; that what is at issue in communist societies today under the name of Fourierism,[1] *embourgoisement,* and even liberalism is nothing other than an orientation to contemporary Western man; that the intense attention to fashion and luxury now prevalent in both individual lives and the system of state production arises from the fact that, practically speaking and in the final analysis, Marxist and capitalist societies present a single kind of man to the marketplace of human history.

Democracy and Western liberalism—whatever sanctity may attach to them in the abstract—are in practice nothing but the free opportunity to display all the more strongly this spirit and to create all the more speedily and roughly an arena for the profit-hungry forces that have been assigned to transform man into an economic, consuming animal.

Thus we have: state capitalism in the name of socialism; governmental dictatorship in the name of "dictatorship of the proletariat"; intellectual tyranny in the name of the one Party; fanaticism of belief in the name of "diamat";[2] and finally,

---

[1] The literal transcription here is "furalism." We also surmise that the word intended might be "formalism." (Tr.)

[2] Diamat: a contraction of "dialectical materialism," the materialism that is supposed to be "the principles of belief to which education of the young,

reliance on the principles of mechanism and economism in the name of quickly attaining "economic abundance in order to pass from socialism to communism"! All are burdens that have befallen humanity in the name of a sacred, free, and creative will and that cast it like a "social artifact" into a crude but all-encompassing organization—that is, into a most blatant state of the same political and intellectual alienation that Marx spoke of in relation to bourgeois man.

The second category of modern calamities is that of ideological calamities. (Here we employ the term "ideology" in its broadest possible sense. The various contemporary ideologies, claiming as they do to be based on contemporary science, all negate the concept of man as a primary being; even those that boast of their humanism do so.)

Historicism presents history as a single determinative material current that in its course constructs out of the material elements, in accordance with the inexorable laws of the historical process, something called man. Thus, in the final analysis, historicism leads to a materialistic determinism in which man is a passive element.

Biologism, which assigns precedence to the laws of nature, regards man just as it regards an animal, but sees him as the latest link in the chain of evolution; otherwise, it looks upon all human spiritual manifestations and unique qualities as occasioned by man's physical constitution, like the natural instincts!

Sociologism views man as a vegetable growing in the garden of his social environment, and thus needing the proper climate and soil; it supposes that only as the garden is changed will the human harvest change, and that, as in the preceding case, this process operates according to scientific laws beyond possible human intervention, laws governing man's actions and even his personality.

If we add to these schools those of materialism and naturalism (which view man as, respectively, a material artifact and

---

scientific research, literature and the arts, philosophy, and the scientific outlook must conform." That is to say, it is a kind of religious rule without religion!

an animal), a picture of the ideological calamities in the present age comes to hand.

In this context, the situation of Marxism is a confused one. Marx in one of his phases is a materialist, and thus in no position to regard the being man as anything but an element within the confines of the material world. (We find him writing to Engels, after studying the works of Darwin, "I accept this view as the biological basis for my philosophy of history.")

In another phase, he is an extreme partisan of sociologism. Thus he grants society its independence vis-a-vis naturalistic and humanistic tendencies and then, by arbitrarily and categorically grouping its elements under the headings of either infrastructure or superstructure (the former representing the mode of material production, and the latter, culture, morals, philosophy, literature, arts, ideology, and so forth), he in effect presents man as equivalent to this superstructure, in that man is nothing more than the sum of these parts. In short, humanity turns out to be the product of the mode of material production. Since Marx also specifies the mode of production as consisting of the tools of production, in the final analysis, the primacy of man in Marxism derives from the primacy of tools; that is, instead of humanism one might speak of "utensilism," or one might say that mankind is not considered, as in Islam, the progeny of Adam, but rather that of tools!

By annexing "dialectical" to "materialism," Marx not only withholds from humanity a crown of glory, but also sets up a materialistic determinism over and above the force of historical determinism in man, which, at the level of practical application, amounts to another chain. For this truly leads to the fettering of the human will, the source of man's primacy in the world, and ultimately plunges humanity into the same pit of fatalism that upholders of superstitious religious teachings (or rather, philosophers and theologians dependent upon the political establishment) dug for it.

The chain is one and the same—its far end now affixed not to the heavens but to the earth. Thus, it is more than a casual slur to refer to this materialism as "fanatical."

WE SEE THAT THE CALAMITY faced by humanity today is first and foremost a human calamity. Humanity is a species in decline; it is undergoing a metamorphosis and, just like a pupating butterfly, is in danger because of the success of its own ingenuity and labors.

What is more astounding, throughout history humanity has usually been sacrificed to the idea of its own deliverance. In a kind of historical reversal, it has been the longing for deliverance that has forged the chains of human captivity and, by offering hope of release, led people into the trap!

Religion, both a powerful love and an invitation to perfection and salvation, after issuing from its primal, limpid springs and coursing through history, underwent a change in its flavor and quality; its course came under the control of those very powers that held the crown of history and that had led in the "social era."

Thus, in China, the school of Lao Tzu at first constituted a summons to deliverance from capitivity in an artificial life, a fragmented intellect, and a rude civilization that drew true man into bondage, distorting and tainting primordial human nature, which in reality accords with the Principial Nature, the Tao. This school of Lao Tzu became in time entangled in the worship of innumerable gods, gods who exploited mankind financially, sapped its intellectual powers, and condemned it to endless fears and obsequies.

Confucius, in order to free the people from the thralldom of those imaginary forces, fought against superstition. He guided the people out of the embrace of senseless fantasies, endless sacrifices, vows, supplications, and debilitating self-mortifications, and toward history, society, life and reason. He set forth the principle termed *li*[3] as the intellectual basis for a rational organization of social life. In later times, however, this same fundamental principle was to take the form of immutable customs subject to an unthinking conformity that killed any sort of social transformation. People grew like the

---

[3] This may be an error for *i*, "morality," as: "The superior man comprehends righteousness [*i*: the "oughtness" of a situation]; the small man comprehends gain [*li*: profit]" (*Analects of Confucius*, 4:16). (TR.)

animals frozen in the polar ice caps; they fell into quiescence and a state of fanatical conservatism. One sociologist noted, "If we see that the society and civilization of China in the course of twenty-five hundred years has neither fallen into utter decline, nor progressed or experienced upheavals, the cause is the conservative and traditionalist rule of the Confucian mind"!

Indian religion, which had within it a clear knowledge of man coupled with a deep understanding of the unity of God, nature, and man—an understanding that infused spirit into the body of the world and served as a force for sublimating the human spirit—was transformed into a horrifying mass of superstitions, in which people were set upon by swarms of untold gods. These gods stole the last crumb of their hapless worshippers and then proceeded to condemn exponents of deliverance (*moksa*) and the high Eastern mysticism (*vidya*) to deadly superstitious austerities and to abject servitude under the official religious establishment.

The Buddha came to deliver the Hindus; he summoned them to freedom from the bondage of worshipping the astral divinities. But *his* followers became Buddha-worshippers, so much so that today, in Persian, the word *bot*, derived from "Buddha," appears in the compound *botparasti* ("idol-worship"), the common expression for the most serious form of *shirk*[4]— that is, idolatry.

The Messiah—the promised Savior—came to deliver humanity from the bonds of materialism and rabbinical ritualism, to free religion from servitude to the merchants and racists of Israel, to establish peace, love, and the salvation of the spirit. Thus he wanted to liberate the peoples who were under the spell of the superstitions of the rabbis and Pharisees and condemned to slavery under the crushing imperialism of Rome. But we have seen how Christianity itself succeeded to the throne of the Roman Empire, with the Roman Church perpetuating the imperial order; how scholasticism came to provide the intellectual underpinnings of medieval feudalism,

---

[4] *Shirk:* making something a "partner" with God; setting something alongside God as worthy of worship. (TR.)

and how it came to murder free thought, free human growth, free science. We have seen how the "religion of peace" spilled blood more freely than any known to previous history, and how, whereas man should have become Godlike (that is, spiritually and morally), God became man-like.

Finally we come to Islam, the last link in the development of the historical religions, which arrived under the standard of *tauhid*[5] and salvation, in order that, in the words of the Muslim soldier, it might summon mankind "from the lowliness of the earth to the heights of the heavens, from servitude to each other to the service of the Lord of the Universe, and from the oppression of the religions to the justice of Islam."[6] We know how it was reshaped under the Arab Caliphate, how it became a rationale for the acts of the most savage conquerors, and how in time it became a powerful cultural force, which, in the name of jurisprudence, scholastic theology, and Sufism, cast an aura of religiosity over the feudal order of the Saljuqs and Mongols and bound the Muslim people in the chains of predestination. The road to salvation was no longer mapped out through *tauhid*, pious acts, and knowledge. Instead, it lay either through an inherited tradition of blind conformity, entreaties, vows, and supplications; or else in flight from reality, society, and life into astral worlds, a way characterized by pessimism concerning human history, progress, and the salvation of man in this world, and the repression of all natural human wants and proclivities.

———

DURING AN AGE in which religion had emerged as a regressive force in relation to scientific and social progress—inhibiting the intellectual, spiritual, and volitional flowering of humanity; giving rise to a mass of formalities, taboos, and

[5] *Tauhid:* the profession of divine unity. (TR.)

[6] This celebrated statement was made by a Muslim soldier in the army that conquered Isfahan, addressing himself to the commander of the Persian garrison. (TR.)

superstitions; presiding through its official custodians, headed by the Church and the Pope, over the fate of ideas and nations —the Renaissance (which we will take to be the upsurge of society's motivating spirit, rather than the rising of the intellectuals), by contrasting the stagnation of the Middle Ages under the rule of the religious custodians to the Golden Age of Greece and Rome, issued a call to freedom to its people through nationalism, as against the Latin imperialism of the papacy, and to humanity at large through science, as against the rigid and superstitious Catholic scholasticism.

What were the watchwords of this upsurge? Human freedom from the bonds of the all-compelling will of heaven, release of the intellect from the dominance of religious belief, release of science from scholastic dogma, a turning from heaven to earth to build the paradise that religion had promised for the hereafter, right here on earth!

What exciting slogans! Freedom of the intellect; science to be our guide; paradise on the spot! But what hands were to build this paradise on earth? Those of colonized nations, exploited human beings, with the assistance of scientific technology.

So we come to science and capital.

Science was freed from subservience to religion only to become subservient to power and at the disposal of the powerful. It was transformed into short-sighted, rigid scientism, which killed the Messiah and became another lackey to Caesar. The machine that was to have been humanity's tool for ruling nature and escaping enslavement to work was transformed into a mechanism that itself enslaved man.

Finally, let us look at the gatekeeper of this paradise: capitalism, but capitalism armed with science and technology—a new magician bewitching humanity into new captivity amid the massive pitiless wheels of mechanism and techno-bureaucracies. And man? An economic animal whose only duty is to graze in this paradise. The philosophy of "consume, consume, consume"!

And the watchwords? Liberalism!—that is, apathy. Democracy!—that is, "Elect those who have already chosen your lot for you." Life? Material existence. Morals? Opportunism and egoism. The goal? Consumption. The philosophy of life? Satiation of the natural appetites. The ultimate aim? A life of leisure and enjoyment. Faith? Ideals? Love? The meaning of existence? The meaning of man? Forget it!

But Adam rebelled, even in this paradise on earth.

MARXISM: the repudiation of capitalism; the repudiation of classes; the repudiation of exploitation, the state, specialization, accumulation of wealth, the ethics of self-seeking—above all, the repudiation of human captivity, that deformation of man's essential nature in the system of production and social order. How marvelous! A society to be founded not simply upon "To each according to his work," but upon "To each according to his needs"!

What does this mean? It means the absolute equality of all people! That is, above and beyond each person's receipt of his due, it promises a society in which each will receive more than what he is owed! A vision? A utopia? No! This time it is not religion speaking of paradise, nor philosophy devising the Virtuous City,[7] nor is it the idealists, the ethical socialist utopians, but rather it is "scientific philosophy" taking on the question.

What hands will construct this ideal society? Well, it is not so much a matter of constructing as of its being constructed—with the discovery of the ineluctable laws of history comes the "good news" that its realization is inevitable! The workers, pressed beyond endurance by poverty and exploitation under capitalism, the intellectuals, in rebellion against the bourgeois

---

[7] The Virtuous City [Madine-ye Fazele]: the concept having its roots in Plato's Republic and in the Muslim philosophy associated most closely with Abu Nasr Mohammad Farabi (874-950), meaning a city that is ruled by sages and whose inhabitants strive to attain true justice, happiness, and perfection. [TR.]

paradise, and the thinkers who envision human liberation—what do they seek?

Once again we find, instead of "the withering away of the state," the dictatorship of the proletariat; instead of "a free society and freedom in one's work," a society completely planned from top to bottom, in which each individual is assigned a role; instead of the elimination of mechanism, greater emphasis placed upon the "revolutionary acceleration of production," itself based on the mechanistic philosophy of capitalism; instead of "human freedom from bourgeois bureaucracy," human captivity in a monolithic governmental bureaucracy; instead of ending the increased human specialization caused by capitalist expansionism, having still more specialization due to governmental expansionism; instead of human liberation from "capitalist economic-administrative organizations," human enslavement to a hyper-organized society; instead of an increase in human freedom, the molding of human society, culture, and morality; instead of blind imitation of, and devotion to, the Church, the very same behavior toward the ideological committee; and instead of the denial of personality in history, the cult of personality. Ideologically speaking, since the fall of humanism at the hands of the base materialism of economism, humanity, having lost its self-aware and sensitive will, which had meant the superior capacity to master existence, has become a pawn in a blind hisical contest and the unwitting product of the material dialectics that governs it!

As we consider capitalism's liberated man and Marxism's man in fetters, capitalism's pseudo-man and Marxism's molded man—can we say which is more tragic?

———————

EXISTENTIALISM revolted against both of these. The humanitarians, who had always sought human freedom and independence, sensed the dangers in the inhuman character of capitalism and mechanism as early as the eighteenth and, more particularly, nineteenth centuries, and began attacking them on aesthetic and moral grounds, as well as on grounds of scientific analysis and logic. Along these lines, they produced a rich and vivid literature, from which Marxism also drew much nourishment. (As Raymond Aron has said, "Marxism is nothing but the intelligent compilation of what non-Marxists have said.")

What is interesting here is that, following the brilliant successes of the capitalist system and its definitive triumph in the blossoming of European civilization, the most advanced of the present age, a considerable and very powerful opposition of the human spirit has been brought to bear against it— to combat it has become the most basic duty of humanitarian intellectuals.

Capital is the producer, capital is the criterion for the value of goods, capital is the repository of truth. Work, this highest manifestation of humanity, is placed at the disposal of capital!

How strange! Capital has become the great idol of our age. Next to it, man is nothing; he is alienated from himself, a mere slave, a votary.

And the other adventure of man's that took shape alongside this was also disastrous and bitter.

Marxism, half a century after the perfection of its ideology, was put into practice in an unexpected quarter, one that certainly would not have been approved of by Marx, as witness his early polemics against Russia. And now we see a new idol. Man, the child of society—so society itself, together with the human mind, conscience, values, morals, culture, ideas, sensibilities—arises from *the means of production*, which today means the machine!

It's the old story of the poet who broke off relations with his beloved to free himself from the dangerous bewitchment of her eyes. To forget her, he devoted himself to horticulture. He hoped to replace his obsession with those mad eyes with this new occupation; however, he complained:

> *Just as the winter clouds have fled,*
> *The coy narcissus ailing lies.*

Its stalks are all in blossoms hid;
In each, alas, I see her eyes.[8]

Those very men who, fleeing mechanism, were caught up in Marxism (which issued the strongest attacks on mechanism), became, after the triumph of that ideology and the rise to power of communist regimes, still more trapped in mechanism. For "material abundance" was proclaimed the essential prerequisite for realizing the ideal communal society, and the prerequisite for this abundance, in turn, was the transformation of society into a massively industrialized system. This transformation would be based on principles that, in Lenin's words, "must be learned from capitalism"!— that is to say, specialization, a typical techno-bureaucratic institutional framework, and competition based upon individual self-interest. Beyond all this, there would be a single organization working rapidly to embrace all members of society and, over it, a new class of rulers consisting of the leading bureaucrats—likewise capitalists!

Isn't Marxism really just the other side of the coin of Western capitalism?

The spirit of human liberation continued to unfold. Especially after World War II, the peoples of Asia and Africa embarked on a path of progressive, anti-colonialist nationalism coupled with a return to their authentic cultural values and renewed contact with their historic roots—a revival of their national characters. Meanwhile, a generation severed from religion, disgusted with capitalist mechanism, and now disillusioned with the promised land of communism, found a breath of fresh air in existentialism. At the heart of it was Sartre, who consciously, powerfully gave expression to the affliction brought on by these calamities.

---

[8] From a Chinese original very capably translated by Hamidi Shirazi, without, of course, any mention of its source!

IN COMPARISON WITH capitalism, which reconstituted man as an economic animal; in comparison with Marxism, which found man an object made up of organized matter(!); in comparison with Catholicism, which saw him as the unwitting plaything of an imperious unseen power (the Divine Will); in comparison with dialectical materialism, which saw him as the unwitting plaything of the deterministic evolution of the means of production—existentialism made man a god! It paid him the grandest worship: "All the beings of this world realize their existence after their essence is determined, except man, who creates his essence subsequent to his existence."

It is clear what the tree or talking parrot will be prior to its existence, but man is the first entity about whom it is unclear: What will he be? What will be become? What will he make of himself? What will he choose for his essence?

Man, therefore, is not God's creation, nor nature's creation, nor is he the offspring of the means of production. Man is a god who creates himself! Given all the disrespect paid man by the Church, capitalism, and communism, it is easy to see what an incentive this call could be to souls believing in the miracle of man!

In our time, it was natural that this call would be made by Sartre, a man who enjoyed the most forceful personality and literary style of all modern philosophers.

Yet Sartre suffers from the same contradictions as Marx, who tries to compel the workers and intellectuals to destroy the capitalist system and begin building a socialist order. That is, he has recourse to human thought, ideas, will, and choice, but at the same time he elaborates a system in which no role remains for a man endowed with those qualities.

In dialectical materialism, qualitative and quantitative change are determined by pre-existing contradictions, operating according to deterministic laws. These laws operate to effect the destruction of capitalism and the realization of communism, which leaves no room for the operation of human choice and responsibility.

Sartre, by distinguishing between what inheres in man and what inheres in nature, admits a dualism. A dualistic cosmogony of the type we see in the "historical" dualism of Zoroaster, the "essential" dualism of Mani, and the "human" dualism of Islam may be explained. But Sartre, coming after Nietzsche, Hegel, and Marx and two centuries after the encyclopedists, cannot, or will not, present himself as a *religious* spirit. He remains loyal to materialism and, in order to show existentialism to be a school in the Marxist tradition, goes so far as to sever it from its roots in Heidegger and graft it onto Marxist stock. He is determined to have it regarded as a post-Marxist school, not a pre-Marxist one. The pitiable decline of his exalted existentialism from the peaks of the "god-man" to the desert of useless anxiety ensues from this.

Is it dialectical materialism or dualism? Materialism is a sort of material monotheism. How, then, has this dualistic *shirk*, this dichotomizing of man and world, entered in?

Sartre (in contrast to Marx, who considers even the most exalted human qualities and the most sacred human ideals outgrowths of the system of production—that is, like goods, arising from the exigencies of technological hardware) proclaims, "If a person born paralytic doesn't become a champion runner, then that individual alone is responsible"!

Bravo! But how is a Marxist to account for this assertion? Faced with the question of where such a supernatural, supra-material will, which can triumph over the social environment and even over the natural human constitution, finds its well-springs, what is the materialist to reply? Has matter itself produced a being that is immaterial?

An affirmative answer by a materialist admits to the occurrence of a miracle and, likewise, to a belief in the creation of the world by an unseen God and a denial of materialism.

The difficulties with Sartre's existentialism, however, do not end at this level of philosophical underpinnings. Rather, a still more serious difficulty arises from the fact that this school centers its full weight on human action, and it is precisely here that it falls lame:

Man makes himself by his own act.

What is meant by "his own act"?

In a word, choice.

What is meant by "choice"?

That to which human free will, itself arising from no external cause, divine or material, relates as a first or independent cause: affirmation or negation.

Here, apart from Sartre's inability to explain how this metaphysical will has sprung into the materialist's universe and entered into the chain of material causation, a greater, indeed a very basic dialectical conflict arises automatically and proves insoluble, and that is that choice, however free and independent, must have some criterion, must take shape on the basis of *values*.

Thus, at this point we see arising that same old question of good and evil, of morals. Of course, Sartre is fully aware of the problem, and addresses it:

What is "good"? What is "evil"?

Dialectical materialism need not answer this question. No determinism need do so, be it theological or materialist, since only in the event of human free choice, with its "what is one to choose?" and "why?", does the issue of responsibility arise.

But Sartre, having carried the question of human choice to its metaphysical zenith, must provide some rule by which to distinguish good and evil; that is to say, he must specify some criterion for the choices human individuals must make in practice.

Heidegger, Sartre's intellectual lodestar, says, "Man is a solitary being hurled into this desert-world." Sartre designates this mode of apprehension *delaissement*, meaning being thrown back upon oneself. This resembles the concept of "assignation" [*tafviz*][9] in our philosophy.

This man, freed from God, nature, and deterministic historical and environmental laws, possessing a quasi-divine free will, is still *responsible* as he puts this free will into practice, but responsible toward what? (This is the second question mark left standing before Sartre!)

He struggles to answer these two questions, but, unfortunately, in neither instance do we see any further evidence of

---

[9] Assignation: the effective delegation to man by God of certain of His functions with respect to the ordering of creation. (TR.)

his great reasoning powers, his sound logic, or his brilliant literary skills.

Sartre makes the principle of *good sense* the criterion of good, which must be affirmed, and evil, which must be rejected: "If in the course of exercising choice an individual feels that this choice should have a general applicability and be imitated by others, then this choice embodies the good. If he feels that only he should act thus, and others should not follow him, the act is evil."

For example: "A butcher who sells meat fraudulently wishes that no one else do this, but when he sells good meat at less than the prevailing rate, he would like to see everyone transact his business in the same way."

So the criterion of good and evil is, first, personal sentiment, and secondly, a totally idealistic matter! How strange that a materialist aligned with Marxism should render such an individualistic and subjectivist account of human behavior!

Could Sartre be unaware that his existentialist morals are so weak and ill-founded and have such unfortunate consequences? Absolutely not!

"There is no other recourse." This is his own answer.

When we start by assuming a materialistic universe, Sartre —along with anyone else who wishes to exalt human freedom and dignity, to deliver it from the grasp of naturalism (the older materialism) or dialectical materialism (the new one), and to have man stand on the two feet of his own free will— inevitably either casts man back into the dungeon of unseeing, unconscious materialistic determinism, or else keeps him standing there, but vain and meaningless, with no purpose, while all human values go tumbling down—and with what terrible speed!

We hear: heaven is idiotic; existence is empty; nature is in blind, determinative motion. Intelligence, feeling, direction, and will are lacking in the universe. Existence has no particular meaning. In this terrible void, man, a stranger, thrown back upon himself, torn free from every bond, is a free will that must create its own meaning, value, goals, and truth.

We see, however, that existentialism has given the individual a sportscar called Will and Freedom, while at the same time whispering in his ear, "There's really nowhere to go. But go wherever you like, knowing that whatever direction you choose, it is your personal choice—nothing more—and is otherwise no different from the direction anyone else would choose, since there is no civilization anywhere." There can be no doubt that such a gift is entirely worthless, and might even be termed a menace!

To make man, like God, a free will that can act in any way it wishes, and then to answer the question "How should he act?" by saying, "However he wishes," is to create a destructive vicious circle.

Sartre, though, has no other recourse since, on the one hand, he accepts dialectical materialism as his world-view, and, on the other, he proclaims human freedom of choice; in such a meaningless and materialistic universe, he can propose no criteria for choice, no standard of values other than personal "good sense."

Sartre is fully aware that his social and moral existentialism may be thus summed up: (1) "You have the ability to accomplish anything." (2) "Whatever you accomplish—if you do it in freedom—is permissible, since outside your choice there exists no criterion that would stand in the way of it."

The conclusion? Therefore, any action whatever is permissible for this free and capable man.

In fact, Sartre himself draws this conclusion. He frequently echoes with approval Dostoevsky's well-known saying, "If we remove God from the universe, every act is permissible for a person."

Finally, as all objective moral criteria and human spiritual values fall away, is it possible that Sartre's existentialism, by proclaiming the human will free and independent in the world and in society, has brought forth, instead of a god, a demon?

Humanity Between Marxism and Religion

IT IS CERTAINLY DIFFICULT these days to speak of religion; the modern mind can hardly accept it as a progressive, liberating force.

What, we must ask ourselves, is this modern mind? Where did it take shape and acquire such an attitude?

It comes from the West, just like the other products and manifestations of the modern life and civilization upon which the West has left its mark. But today, in the intellectual milieu of the East, when the "West" is mentioned, the word brings to mind only capitalism, industrialism, Christianity, colonialism, bourgeois liberalism.

When the intention is to deny the West, to resist it, Marxism is considered the most effective weapon against it; whereas it is seldom realized that Marxism itself is utterly a product of the history, social organization, and cultural outlook of this same West. This is not simply because its founders and leading figures are all Western, but rather, to employ a Marxist analysis, the ideology itself must be accounted a mere superstructure resting on the social infrastructure of the bourgeois industrial system of production in the modern West.

Marxism dogmatically divides society into two parts, infrastructure and superstructure. It equates the former with the "mode of production," which is determined in accordance with the nature of the "means of production." The form of the superstructure—which comprises religion, morals, literature, arts, psychology, philosophy; political, social, economic, humanistic, and existential thought and belief, and so forth, to every shade of ideology—then arises from the means of production.

49

Given this *a priori* principle and method of perception, who could doubt that, for capitalism and Marxism alike, the means of production are and have been the same?

It is also appropriate to mention here that, for Protestantism and for Fascism, the means of production have also been the same.

Protestantism, capitalism, Marxism, and Fascism? These four are brothers born of the same materialism and raised in the same household, the West, although they have followed four different careers.

Protestantism is a religion, but one that turned from love to power; from Christianity it has forged an ideology and morality compatible with bourgeois life.

Capitalism advertised as its official ideology the liberalism and democracy based on the seventeenth-century materialism of the encyclopedists and assembled from concepts of freedom and human dignity in philosophy and science—an ideology amenable to the new bourgeoisie.

Marxism, with its economic rationale for all manifestations of human existence, for human life and history, turned socialism into a purely economic order based on "material abundance through industry" and forged from Hegel's dialectic (which found God realized in human history) the means to realize a bourgeois life for the proletariat!

Fascism, arising in the same social setting as Marxism, was basically a movement of the technocrats and bureaucrats, who, between the two focal points of power—capital and labor—lacked the least foothold and were mere pawns of these forces. Thus they sought power and rule. Fascism mobilized large numbers from among the middle classes.

What is held in common by these four movements—one a religion, another an economic system, the third a revolutionary class ideology, and the last a virulent racism? All four favor:

(1) The dismissal or categorical denial of any immaterial, spiritual dimension in man; banishment of the notion of man as a being having a supra-material essence, as an inherently idealistic being.

(2) The confinement of human needs and ideals to the narrow limits of material consumption and power, and the triumph of economic needs over all others.

(3) The gravitation of philosophy, or at any rate morals and psychology, toward materialism.

(4) Reliance upon the machine as the sole guarantee of economic power and consumption. Worship of production and, in consequence, assumption by the machine of the role of idol of the new civilization.

(5) Inevitably, a confrontation with religious faith, or the spiritual dimension of religion, which is considered the most powerful obstacle and source of resistance to these movements.

Protestantism, formerly a reformist movement (within the framework of Christianity) in favor of the new bourgeois class, remained within the confines of that class and was unable to become a world-wide intellectual movement.

Then more recently in the fossilized society of the West, the existential philosophy, which once showed itself to be a vital movement and summons, has been abandoned.

Fascism declined as swiftly as it was born; anyway, it is essentially a specific ideological school that amounts to nothing in relation to the scope of world history we are examining here.

Capitalism, in the first place, has changed greatly since the nineteenth century, and in the second, does not constitute a systematic ideological school but rather an economic and social order, which confronts religion only indirectly. That is, anti-religious thinkers combat religion in the name of science, not in the name of capitalism and the bourgeoisie, although such thinkers were nurtured and raised by that social organization and the science upon which they lean is infused with the new bourgeois spirit.

As for Marxism, however: (1) because it has a global mission with no particular religious, cultural, or national confines; (2) because it is a comprehensive, well-defined ideology, committed to the ardent defense of solidly crystallized dogmas; (3) because it not only sets forth a particular economic or political system, but also intrudes into every area, every dimension of the private and social existence of man: material, spiritual, intellectual, and moral; (4) because it possesses a philosophical and credal foundation upon which it bases all of its analyses of, and solutions for, every question of man and society, past and future; (5) because its foundation, dialectical materialism, bears such a clear and undeniable resemblance to the most virulent forms of religious fanaticism; (6) because dialectical materialism, according to the Marxists, is not merely a philosophical perspective like those of the secular materialists and naturalists of ancient Greece or the eighteenth century (which conveyed only a certain philosophical abstraction of man and the universe), but rather is both "the only completely scientific description of reality" and a fanatically pursued mission, incapable of tolerating any other perspective alongside it; (7) because it accounts itself the absolute and exclusive truth, beside which there can be only "absolute falsity"—for these reasons, with all the fervor of a prophetic mission, Marxism sees its task as the systematic eradication of all forms of religion. Since it basically considers religion something not only futile but intellectually damaging, it sees it as an enemy of the people, an obstacle in its path, and it never attempts to conceal the frank words of Lenin: "One must treat religion ruthlessly!"

FOR THE PHILOSOPHICAL BASIS of Marxism's anti-religious outlook, we must look to the works of the intellectuals that Marxists regard as belonging to the new bourgeoisie! Thus, Marx and, following him, Lenin advise that communists republish all the works of the encyclopedists and Feuerbach. (The latter is the connecting link between Hegel's idealism and Marx's dialectical materialism. He is responsible for that "overturning of the Hegelian pyramid" that Marx and Engels claim to have originated, and many of his discussions are to be found uncredited among the pages of their works. He offered an interpretation of religion to which Marx and his followers have added nothing but detail and commentary, or mere repetition.)

The well-known charge laid against religion that turns on "the alienating effect of religion," proclaimed as a great Marxist discovery, is essentially Feuerbach's. In his book *The Essence of Christianity*, he executed the famous inversion wrought upon the school of Hegel in connection with the relation between the Son (Christ) and the Father (God). He says:

> In this instance, it is the Father who is born of the Son. God does not manifest Christ; Christ manifests God, and the Christ who becomes God is himself the outward realization of the human spirit, the spirit of mankind urgently seeking deliverance. The Holy Spirit is none other than that human spirit which, failing to recognize godhood within itself, personifies it in a metaphysical being, and situates what is within itself in an imagined heaven.

This is what he means by the alienating effect of religion; if one can avoid this alienation, one will arrive at oneself, experiencing the self-awareness of *Homo homini deo* ("man who is his own god").

Marx was the son of a Jew who, because of the legal restrictions on daily life for the Jews in Germany, had converted to Protestantism. While a young Hegelian, Marx wrote in the preface to a treatise, "Philosophy is allied with the faith of Prometheus; in sum, I feel a loathing toward the gods. . . . All the proofs of God's existence prove rather His non-existence. . . . The real proofs should have the opposite character: 'Because nature lacks a right order, God exists'; 'because an unintelligible world exists, God exists' . . . in other words, irrationality is the basis for God's existence."[1]

Who is Prometheus? In Greek mythology, he is one of the gods, who, in order to render a service to man, betrayed the other gods. One night as all the gods slept, he stole the divine fire and handed it over to man. When the other gods came to

---

[1] *Difference Between the Democritean and Epicurean Philosophy of Nature*, doctoral dissertation written between 1840 and March 1841. Marx's discussion beginning with "All the proofs . . ." actually appears in the appendix to this document. (TR)

know of this, they bound him in chains. They were alarmed that humanity should possess the celestial fire, for they wanted people to remain forever in darkness and base weakness, never to ascend to a station near that of the angels.

Marx, who had taken up the Promethean faith and the idea of a Promethean society from the humanistic sociologists, and who was to be influenced by Saint-Simon and later by Proudhon, has in this instance inherited the religious outlook of Greek mythology, just as they did. He has generalized from the God-man relationship in Greek religion to that in all religions, unaware that the outlook of the great Eastern religions is completely contrary to it. They envision a God very sympathetic toward humanity, not one, as in the Greek religion, who regards man as a rival and faces him with jealousy and malevolence, only to be met with fear. The religious message of the East is based on the raising of man from earth to heaven, from the ranks of the corporeal and bestial to the angelic or divine. In the religion of Zoroaster, humans fight side by side with the Amshaspands for the victory of Ahuramazda; these supernatural beings are always the patrons of man. In Manichean dualism, it is through man that Divine Light is realized in existence. In Chinese and Indian mysticism, essentially, there exists no impassable barrier between man and God; rather God flows through man and even nature as the Spirit of Being and the Essence of the Real. Most importantly, that divine fire has entered the Jewish, Christian, and Islamic religions (which share a common world-view) in the form of the forbidden tree, with Prometheus becoming Satan, while it is God Who is man's real Prometheus!

When Marx declares, "I feel a loathing toward the gods," we should reflect on his choice of wording. In the preface to a philosophical treatise, indeed one discussing the gods, the choice of the word "loathing" is not a natural one. It expresses an emotion, not a philosophical or scientific point. One must search for the roots of such a reaction in Marx's private life, in the disappointments in love the priests caused him!

Let us look at the rest of his comment: "The real proofs should have the opposite character: 'Because nature lacks a right order, God exists'; 'because an unintelligible world exists, God exists' . . . in other words, irrationality is the basis for God's existence." It exhibits a kind of confused logic in that it has taken the view of popular religion as the criterion of religious reasoning, whereas the popular religious approach always seeks God outside natural, rational laws, in unintelligible courses of events; it sees proofs of His existence in extraordinary occurrences and in unscientific and unnatural sources. By contrast, the scriptures, and particularly the Qur'an, have made a rational case for *tauhid* on the basis of nature, custom, the constant laws of life, and the ordered and intelligible quality of events in the universe. They look upon these things as objective attestations to the existence of an Intelligence Who rules over nature.

The Holy Qur'an harshly criticizes the materialists, asking, "Do you imagine the order of this world to be futile?" It proclaims in answer, *"We did not create heaven, earth, and all between them in vain"* (38:27). Furthermore, God does not set the affairs of the world in motion without their proper causes. Everything rests solidly on God's *sunnah* [wont] in the world: *"You will find no change in God's sunnah"* (35:43). Everything in nature, man, and history has a known quantity and a fixed term. The most important evidences for God's existence offered in the Qur'an point to the existence of a rational order and intelligence in nature.

At this point, we can see how, like a bigoted medieval schoolman, or a political blackmailer, Marx sets up the most deviant, vulgarized, and least widely held views of a rival school of thought as straw men to attack and ridicule.

The only straightforward analysis that Marx offers concerning the origins of religion is his famous assertion: "Man is the author of religion, not religion the author of man." Even here, he is only repeating Feuerbach; he attempts to gain credit for the point by substituting "religion" for "God," and thereby renders it meaningless, or at least obscure. (What does it mean—"Religion is not the author of man"? Has anyone said, "Religion *is* the author of man"?)

Marx says later:

> Religion constitutes a form of self-awareness for those who have not yet gained self-mastery, or who have lost themselves again. Religion is, however, a supra-rational realization of human destiny, for human destiny has no real existence. In consequence, to combat religion is to combat a world for which religion is the spiritual essence.
>
> The affliction of religion simultaneously expresses actual misery and constitutes a protest against it. Religion is the sigh of a helpless entity, the heart of a heartless world, and the spirit of a dispirited being. It [religion] is the opium of the people.
>
> Criticizing religion inevitably leads to criticizing the sea of tears over which religion is the halo.

Where in all this is a thought that does not carry more of literary technique than philosophical depth? If the perspectives that are essentially Feuerbach's are set aside, what remains of Marx but style?

At the close of this discussion, when he assumes a more serious and rational tone, he merely repeats in a fuzzy way Feuerbach's theme of combating the alienating effect of religion: "Criticizing religion delivers man from error, so he may think, act, and create his own reality as one who, having seen through his own error, masters his own intellect . . . that he may revolve around himself, that is, around his own true sun."[2] Is this anything other than that selfsame "atheistic humanism" that is the basis of Feuerbach's position?

"Religion is . . . a supra-rational realization of human destiny." What does this mean?

Marx is no doubt referring to the vulgarized and erroneous notions of the religious thinkers who envision the next world as a substitute for this one with all its economic and human shortcomings. But, on the contrary, anyone who has studied the original scriptural sources and the more conscious exponents of a religion has seen that religion regards the next world as simply the logical and intelligible continuation of life in this world. There is nothing supra-rational or contrary

---

[2] *Contribution to the Critique of Hegel's Philosophy of Law*, written in spring and summer, 1843. (TR.)

to science about it. Heaven and hell, the higher and lower degrees of the afterlife, reflect the respective services or disservices done by each person for his society. They constitute the final outcome of the material and worldly life of an individual (or a collectivity) who in this life has either chosen the road of human progress, grown in moral virtues, and imparted them to the people, or else corrupted his own nature and spread corruption about him.

We see that to perceive the workings of the universe as "unintelligible," "supra-rational," or even unscientific is to lose sight of this reflection and this continuity. It is this that confounds humanity in what Marx calls a "heartless world" and a "dispirited" existence; such is life for the man who, in a world of unfeeling matter, has become the plaything of a blind and unending dialectical conflict and is drowning in a "sea of tears," with his disheartening black halo of atheism.

As we look back on this fanatical and unmitigated attack of Marx on religion, we should note his remark "Religion is a supra-rational realization of human destiny, for human destiny has no real existence." Of course Marx wrote this a century ago, before the advent of the twentieth century and, more especially, the pessimistic age that followed World War II, so he could not see to what results, what wholesale disasters, his words would lead.

"Human destiny has no real existence"—it is precisely here that we have the fundamental difference between religion and materialism.

THAT TODAY HUMANITY SHOULD RUSH toward futility, that the young should engage in pointless rebellion, and that philosophy, art, and literature should speak of the meaninglessness of everything, including the meaninglessness of humanity—these are the natural and inevitable consequences of denying a theistic world-view. That is because to deny God and His presence in existence and man renders existence idiotic and man purposeless, so that neither Sartre's existentialism nor an upside-down Hegelian dialectic via Marx can bestow meaning and intelligence upon them.

It is not surprising that after the fall of the bourgeoisie and the triumph of communism, Marx's dialectics should cease to be operative in history, and the struggle of thesis and antithesis should culminate in a sort of peaceful coexistence! Marx is powerless to indicate where, beyond communism, human destiny should lead in this world here, not to mention the next. That is a question that neither the ancient materialism nor dialectical materialism can answer, since, as Rene Guenon said, "When the world is without meaning and purpose, man is likewise meaningless, purposeless." Marx grants that such a humanity lacks a "real" destiny.

Islam, on the other hand, goes beyond granting humanity an honored place in nature ("We have honored the progeny of Adam," 17:70). It does more than deny that God has made man a helpless creature who, having lost himself, searches for his own values and powers in God's being and demands them from Him with "sighs" and "tears." It holds that God has consigned His trust to humanity: "We offered the trust to the heavens, the earth, and the mountains, and they refused to bear it, fearing it, and man undertook it" (33:72). It holds that humanity was created as God's deputy in nature: "Truly I am about to place on the earth a vice-regent" (2:30). Nothing could go further to confute Marx's and Feuerbach's reasoning in deducing man's alienation from himself before God than the saying of Sayyidna Ali, upon whom be peace, which stands as a decisive affirmation of man's nobility and man's responsibility for his own self-perfection and liberation: "Your disease is within you and you know not, and your remedy is within you and you see not"!

It appears that Marx's knowledge of religion was confined to what his father (of Jewish descent, Protestant by conversion) had comprehended of it. He had not even heard of one of the most basic doctrines of Judaism, Protestant Christianity, and Islam alike: God's assignation of free will to man, that he might struggle in his earthly life and search for his own liberation.

At any rate, when Marx attacks a particular school, rather than base his arguments on its principles of faith and original texts, he reasons from the deviations and superstitions that have overtaken the more degraded and illiterate of its followers, since they make easy targets for ridicule and are readily discredited, and since he thereby frees himself from the need to research further.

Marx seeks the easy way out when he attacks religion, although it changes the tone of his discourse from that of a learned philosopher to that of an evangelist preacher, or a sophist politician. No matter, since for him the attack on religious faith blazes the trail for the victory of Marxism; and, of course, this movement holds that the end justifies the means, even if they include what Lenin terms "ruthlessness toward religion"! It is not surprising, then, that Marx, a "scientific philosopher of dialectics," should, in combating religion scientifically, replace the intellectual and scientific facts concerning religion with "the historical and social role of the religious-minded," and that he should, through the simple expedient of attacking the latter, seek the not-so-easy object of annulling the former.

And thus he would reason that religion is a means for justifying social injustice. At this juncture, he neither enters into a philosophical discussion or scientific inquiry (as the seventeenth-century materialists or even the ancient naturalists did), nor even speaks of religion *per se* or of the original and authentic religious movements:

> The *social principles of Christianity* rationalized ancient slavery, endorsed medieval serfdom, and understand how, when the necessity arises, to support the suppression of the proletariat, however regretfully.
>
> The *social principles of Christianity* preach the necessity for the existence of a ruling class and a ruled class.... The social principles of Christianity relegate compensation for all atrocities to the next world, while explaining their persistence in this world as punishment for original sin, or as a burden God has imposed as a test of His servants. The social principles of Christianity preach dishonor, contemptibility, abjectness, servility, humility—in short, all base qualities. The proletariat, refusing to accept this

debasement, has much greater need of courage, self-respect, pride, and desire for independence, than of bread.
The social principles of Christianity are hypocritical, but the proletariat is revolutionary.[3] (Emphasis added.)

Is this speaker the Karl Marx who supposes morals are the superstructure arising from the economics of production? Is this the Karl Marx who does not distinguish between "ideology" and "organization"? Both suppositions are quite difficult to believe.

Unfortunately, however, this is the Karl Marx who identifies the Messiah with the Pope, so that all non-Marxist intellectuals and even independent Christian thinkers should join in attacking him, regardless of the weakness of this line of his reasoning.

Furthermore, this kind of argument and inference belongs to the vulgar, although unscrupulous propagandists may make use of it for political or quasi-religious ends. It is vulgar to criticize the weakness and corruption of the religious classes and to infer from it that religious studies are futile. To identify the role in society played by the Christian clerical class in the Middle Ages with that of Jesus, the Messiah, in the Palestine of two thousand years ago is, if not highly tendentious, indicative of utter ignorance. To identify the hundreds of thousands of martyrs among the peoples of Palestine, Ethiopia, and Northern and Western Europe who rose against the expansionist Roman imperialism with the nightmarish apparatus that brought about the slaughter of hundreds of thousands of the world's peoples, Christian and non-Christian alike, amounts to nothing more than hollow abuse. Could Marx actually not know that independent Christian thinkers, in struggling against the Church and the clergy (and against what Marx terms "the social principles of Christianity"), have made greater sacrifices, to greater effect, than materialists and Marxists? The 300,000 in Barcelona alone who were massacred by the Church were themselves all Christians! In the case of

---

[3] "The Communism of the *Rheinischer Beobachter*," dated September 5, 1847. (Tr.)

the Hundred Years' War, were they not Christians who were being slaughtered by other Christians?

And why should Marx, like the priests, seek to impugn Islam by making much of the disgraces of the Caliphate? Weren't the first and most outstanding of those martyred by the Caliphate likewise the first and most outstanding of those brought up within the Islamic religion?

It is not surprising that Marx, in order to attack religion, should assume the very tone of the most fanatical religious propagandists attacking an "enemy" religion. What is surprising is that (if the text at hand is studied closely) he has assumed the tone proper to religion! ". . . dishonor, contemptibility, abjectness, servility, humility—in short all base qualities. The proletariat, refusing to accept this debasement, has much greater need of courage, self-respect, pride, and desire for independence, than of bread"—what a remarkable thing! We hear those moral values and spiritual virtues that religion has always defended proclaimed with such fervor by that selfsame Marx who deems them social mores arising from a particular economic system and productive infrastructure, who calls them all mutable, with nothing sacred about them. How is it that here he holds these spiritual values higher than bread? And not for the aristocracy or the bourgeoisie, or from the standpoint of moral idealism, but *for the proletariat!*

Although we do not wish to deny that atrocities may be attributed to the medieval clergy, for one who is cognizant of morals and their relation to religion, who is aware of the way religion has always placed its heaviest reliance upon moral values and has eulogized them, and who likewise has read Plekhanov's essays on communism and morals, to hear Marx say such a thing is astonishing. Spiritual values higher than bread!

Isn't this borrowing the armaments of religion to use in a "ruthless" attack on religion?

MARXISM WAGES WAR on religion more fiercely than do any other of the materialist schools, although to the same extent that it is the most harsh and fanatical of them, it uses the weakest, most ill-founded and ambiguous logic for its attacks. All at the same time, Marxism, like the scientists and the materialist idealists of recent centuries (particularly the seventeenth), regards religion as having arisen due to man's ignorance of the scientific laws of causality; like the materialist psychologists, as a product of man's psychological weakness and lack of self-awareness and self-mastery; like the materialist sociologists, as a carry-over from pre-technological and pre-industrial systems of production and also, most naively and superficially, a cunning strategem of the ruling class to rationalize oppression of the ruled, the people! We see that Marxism makes use of all the anti-religious arguments brought forward to its day from earlier times and adds nothing original to them.

This is an important point to recall concerning the relationship of Marxism and religion. It is considered that Marxism, because it is founded upon dialectical materialism, is in basic conflict with religion, the essence of which rests upon worship of the unseen and the divine world-view. If such be the case, the divergence between Marxism and religion will never remain within the confines of a difference of philosophical and scientific viewpoints, as is true of the discrepancy between religion and Hegel's atheistic idealism, Sartre's materialistic existentialism, or, say, the atheistic humanism of Diderot and Ernest Renan.

On the contrary, Marxism assumes such a militantly hostile stance toward religion that as recently as 1961, more than one hundred years after the birth of Marx, the text of the official program of the Soviet state and Communist Party reaffirms the "protracted and relentless combat against religious faith" in order to establish communism among the Soviet people.

That it should assume such a harshly bellicose stance against religion stems not only from the discrepant philosophies of materialism and religion, but also from the radical difference deriving from two opposed conceptions of human-ity, which give rise in turn to two opposed conceptions of morals, life, economics, culture, education—of man's escha-tological and historical destiny, of society and the universe as a whole.

We should mention another crucial point here. There are those who imagine that of the various religions, Islam, apart from its opposition to Marxism over the question of God, resembles it in many aspects of its approach to human and social questions. These similarities have been discussed to varying extents by such persons as Michel Aflaq, Omar Uzghan, Bashir Muhammad, Bashir Ali, and in the West by Maxime Rodinson. And it is very interesting that, at the oppo-site pole, certain colonial politicians, including some who officiated over massacres in colonized Muslim lands in Africa like General Salan and General Charbonneau in Algeria, have leveled the same accusation against Islam!

To begin with, one may find shared elements in any opposing schools of thought: between German fascism and Jewish Zionism, between materialist humanism and sacred mysti-cism, and in particular between communism and capitalism!

Secondly, similarities of ideal are typically confused with ideological similarities. Opposing ideologies may hold shared ideals. Civilization, scientific progress, and material pros-perity are ideals that a colonized society may struggle to realize, but it must not be forgotten that these amount to the very ideology of the colonialists; that is, they believe that by being colonized by an advanced society, a backward society may achieve civilization, scientific and technological prog-ress, and material well-being. Thus shared ideals may be found in the two diametrically opposed ideologies of coloni-alism and the liberation movements.

Human ideals transcend ideology as well as the limits of the social order and the historical period. They arise from what is specifically human; they form the eternal moral values in man. Freedom from compulsion, growth toward perfection, justice, truth, human self-awareness, the prece-dence of society over the individual; a common measure for value and achievement; the banishment of force, of war, of exploitation, of enslavement, ignorance, and weakness; the rightful chance to live and grow; the elimination of class conflict, of racial, familial, or other collective forms of exclusion, and of unfair social, economic, and moral distinctions —all are human ideals that, throughout the history of human social life, have been the slogans of free and humane people. One might say they constitute the genuine and original basis of humanism in its most general sense. It is from this point on that divergences arise in the various systems of thought, each generating a separate school in the course of interpreting those ideals and, more particularly, the means for their attainment: the religions, through joining humanity to the Origin of the world; philosophy, through disclosing the intelligible laws governing life; Western bourgeois liberalism, by individuals' free and competitive efforts in the field of material production, leading to the acquisition of power, to progress and the development of science; Marxism, by means of state ownership and rule, to a similar outcome; Sufism, through turning to one's self, for the sake of growth in spirit, intellectual self-sufficiency, and deliverance of the spirit from the bonds of the natural appetites; naturalism, on the contrary, through accordance with the qualities of nature; and so forth.

We must now ask, What methods, what systems, do Islam, Christianity, Hinduism, Hegelian idealism, Marxist dialectics, and the others offer for achieving these eternal human ideals?

The question having been asked, we must say truthfully that, contrary to the beliefs of those who look for shared modalities in Islam and the communism of Marx, these, as two comprehensive ideologies, are altogether opposed. As it happens, we must seek to demonstrate this opposition by reference to those same matters in which some persons have seen a similarity! This is due to the fact that the only comparable modality of the two schools is that each is a complete, comprehensive ideology.

The other ideologies for the most part are partial; that is, they are based primarily on a single field of human activity.

For instance, that of materialism and of naturalism is philosophy, while in the fields of politics, economics, morals, sociology, anthropology, and historiography, adherents are given free rein: they may belong to the left or the right; they may consider history methodical and scientific or unmethodical and unscientific; they may account man a being endowed with an essence of a special innate character, or they may regard him as something produced from and shaped by nature, culture, or the means of production. The same may be said of existentialism, to the extent that an existentialist may be a believer or an atheist, socialist or capitalist. Nationalism rests upon the drive for the political independence and cultural integrity of the nation in question; a nationalist may honestly profess idealism or materialism, fascism or democratic ideals, piety or atheism. The same applies to the religions, in that they are based upon man's relationship with the unseen or the sacred. Their rules and ordinances stem from the desire to order this relationship, or from the moral and pedagogical values that safeguard the special life and character of the religion for its adherents.

Islam and Marxism, however, are two ideologies that embrace every dimension of human life and thought, which is to say that each possesses a particular cosmology, a particular code of morals, a particular form of social organization, a particular philosophy of history and future outlook, and a particular vision of what man is and particular means of disseminating that vision. Each is keenly interested in the private and social lives of people in this world. But in all of these areas the two ideologies are diametrically opposed.

Islam and Marxism completely contradict each other in their ontologies and cosmologies. Briefly, Marxism is based on materialism and derives its sociology, anthropology, ethics, and philosophy of life from materialism. The Marxist cosmos, i.e., the materialist cosmos, is, as Marx puts it, a "heartless and dispirited world" where man lacks a "real" destiny. By contrast, the cosmology of Islam rests upon faith in the unseen—the unseen [ghayb] being definable as the unknown actuality that exists beyond the material and natural phenomena that are accessible to the senses and to our intellectual, scientific, and empirical perception, and which constitutes a higher order of reality and the central focus of all the movements, laws, and phenomena of this world.

The Qur'an, at the beginning of the first *surah, al-Baqarah*,[4] proclaims faith in the unseen to be the prerequisite for guidance and the very source of piety: *"A.L.M. This is the Book in which is no doubt, a guide to the pious, who believe in the Unseen* [bi'l-ghayb], *are steadfast in prayer, and spend out of what We have provided for them"* (2:1-2). This "Unseen" is in truth the absolute Spirit and Will of existence. Contrary to idealism, which looks upon the phenomena of the material world as arising from the idea, and in contrast to materialism, which imagines the idea as springing from the material world, Islam regards matter and idea as differing manifestations [*ayat*] of the unseen absolute Being, thus negating both materialism and idealism. It likewise grants the existence of the natural world separate from our idea of it and also maintains that man, as a being in which the idea subsists, has an independence and a nobility relative to material nature, society, and production.

Marx strives, in imitation of Feuerbach and the other new humanists, to free humanity from life as an economic entity and from intellectual and political alienation from itself; tries to restore its unity by banishing divisive specialization; wishes, as he puts it, to "return humanity to its human values, innate powers, and self-mastery"; and would have it achieve self-awareness and become free of all compulsion. In failing to perceive in his cosmology any factor other than matter and its unseeing, unconscious conflict, he necessarily plunges the humanity he has exalted in his ideology into the pit of insensate matter and, in the final analysis, ranks it among natural objects.

In fact, Marx suffers from the same contradictions that all materialist thinkers do who attempt to rise to the defense of humanism. Having maintained that there is only one princi-

---

[4] Strictly speaking, the second. [TR.]

ple of existence, matter, they struggle in vain as humanists to accept a second, humanity. Therefore, from a certain standpoint, when they first speak of unity in relation to being, and then introduce the concept of humanism, they are faced with dualism—since one may not both profess materialism and, by extricating humanity from the world of material things, bestow a primacy and independence upon it.

But the idealists who believe in humanism are also involved in troubles. Those who either deny the actuality of the external world or negate its validity as it is perceived, granting primacy to the idea (with a human intelligence), certainly affirm humanism or the primacy of man. Yet, by denying the actuality of the material world and denying science (the bridge between the idea and the actual), they abandon man as a primary being for a mind taken out of the world of actuality and placed in a melancholy world with absolutely no criterion for distinguishing true from false, knowledge from ignorance, good from evil, real from imaginary. Like the Sophists of ancient Greece, they inevitably end up in the lap of a kind of egocentrism. And is humanism nothing more than an egocentrism?

So we see that man turns out to be an object in Marxist humanism, and in idealistic humanism, a jinn! Islam, however, not only resolves the oppositions of nature, man, and God through the principle of *tauhid*, but also, by proclaiming the truth that human subjectivity and material nature are both different signs or manifestations of a single sublime essence, transcends the oppositions of idea and matter, and of man and nature. Even while considering the essential human reality and material actuality as two distinct principles, it establishes a fundamental bond, an existential relation, between them, in regarding the two as arising from a single origin.

Not only does the notion of religion's alienating effect, which Marx borrowed from Feuerbach and relies so heavily upon, have no applicability to Islam, but the opposite is true: man's alienation from himself before God is replaced by man's awareness of himself in relation to himself! To demonstrate the point, let us retrace first Feuerbach's and then Marx's reasoning (then their conclusions will be easily refuted): God is a human fabrication. God is a manifestation of human nature; man has projected his own essential values and powers onto heaven and undertaken to worship them in the form of a transcendental being called God; in truth he has attributed to this object of worship what he himself possesses, which exists within him.

If we accept this position, then we have refuted the concept of man's alienation from himself, since in this case "God" becomes synonymous with "man." "Theolatry" turns out to be "anthropolatry," and man's alienation from himself through God is transformed into his alienation from himself through the human.

In addition, isn't this human awareness of itself in relation to itself, or human self-awareness, another way of saying "humanism"? If so, "theolatry" would characterize a religion in which man, in a material world constantly threatening him with materialism, animal degradations, and moral lapses, would be the devoted worshipper of his own transcendental sacred values! We see that in Marx's most forceful attack upon religion, his logic overturns his own conclusions!

As it happens, to conclude that "theolatry" in its developed, conscious form neither negates man's primacy nor produces in man alienation from himself, but in fact does bestow primacy on man and sanctity on human values and expresses an exalted, meaningful, and worthwhile humanism—to do this is to reach a conclusion altogether in accord with Islam.

As opposed to the view of the Catholics or the Sufis, who acknowledge an opposition between God and man (i.e., who make man an "extinction" [fana] in the face of eternity [baqa] and present him as condemned to divine predestination), in Islam, through the principle of assignation (i.e., humanity's assumption of its freedom, discretionary powers, and destiny), man is free of material determination and divine foreordination. We even see Adam in God's paradise rebelling against His command. This free will empowered to choose makes man God's vice-regent in nature. When man has attained this divine rank in nature (despite the materialists' efforts to deify man, as Marx saw it, the materialist world-view is too narrow and petty to envision such a thing), God has all the angels prostrate themselves before him and makes all the powers of nature subject to him.

We see that man in the Islamic world-view is a governing will in relation to nature, and might be termed the god of nature; in relation to God, he fulfills the role of His vice-regent. We see how foreign what Marx termed the "affliction of religion" is to the conceptions that make up the text of the Qur'an.

The most important factor prompting Marx to say "I loathe God" is the principle of worship and obedience inhering in the relation between God and man. In contrast to Marx, however, who infers this principle from its corrupted and vulgarized forms, prevalent among the backward and superstitious, and sees in it a manifestation of man's misery, affliction, and alienation from himself, Islam, in God's words, interprets it as a factor for the growth and perfection of the divine nature in mankind: "Obey Me, My servant, so that I may make you like Me."

We see that in the philosophy of Islam, the relation of God and man is one of reciprocity, where self-knowledge and knowledge of God come to be synonymous, or, alternatively, where the former functions as a preliminary to the latter. We refer here to the profound remark of the Iranian mystic [Bayazid Bestami]: "For years I sought God and found myself; now that I seek myself, I find God."

Quite to the contrary of the views of Feuerbach and Marx, it is not humanity that has made God, reposed its proper values in Him, and now worships Him; it is rather God Who has made humanity, reposed His proper values in it, and now praises it! Accordingly, if Marx, instead of speaking of man's alienation from himself vis-a-vis God, had discussed God's alienation from Himself vis-a-vis humanity(!), at least his remarks would have been interesting as a sort of philosophical satire.

It may be seen that we are no longer speaking of the contradiction between religion and materialism, or between Islam and dialectical materialism, but rather of the question of humanity. Every ideology, religious or anti-religious, necessarily revolves around the question of the human, and it is in fact at this point that Marxism most diverges from Islam. This ever-increasing divergence is the natural result of the two opposed world-views from which the two ideologies arise, and which underlie their whole manner of interpreting phenomena. From this point on, Islam and Marxism prove incompatible in all areas of politics, economics, ethics, and social concerns. Islam interprets and evaluates man on the basis of *tauhid,* and Marxism does so on the basis of production [*taulid*].

Marx is undoubtedly aware that he thus vitiates all the moral values and humanistic qualities of man that he so fervently praised in some of his own writings, since in one swoop he transfers all the values that humanity has created, or at any rate possesses, to the means of production, which makes the primacy of man, in the Marxists' version, a primacy of economic tools. Within the narrow bounds of the impoverished materialist world-view, no element is more honored than that of production.

Thus we see that, both in theory and in practice, Marx's communism, while trying to justify itself on the basis of the highest moral values and human ideals and while presenting itself as the very realization of humanism, quickly degenerates into an economism.

If Stalinism, in its obsession with the economy and fanatical drive to increase production, has been accused of plotting a deviationist course, the same could not be said of Lenin. Virtually all the authorities agree that he faithfully pursued and realized a Marxist policy. It is no accident that the first years of the Soviet revolution see him making heavy industry the cornerstone of the revolution, proclaiming the economic abundance thus to be created as the fundamental condition for realizing the Marxists' ideal society (the ultimate goal of communism), and to this end relying on the following three principles:

1. Rapid industrialization, with principal reliance on the establishment of heavy industries;

2. Comprehensive planning, with the lives of all members of society to be minutely coordinated by a techno-bureaucratic organization (in this, "one must," Lenin himself put it, "imitate capitalism");

3. The institution of competition as a means to increased production; this to be through the establishment of a set of models for, and stimuli to, individual and collective effort via the stimulation of self-interest, in the form of unequal wages and rewards, and material and occupational incentives for the technically skilled and the administratively competent.

We see that what many writers, including large numbers of communists, have attacked as the "Stalinist economy" was based on the policies of Lenin. It must be added that Lenin was thus realizing the scheme Marx and Engels had proclaimed as the method for constructing the ideal society!

How is it that "justice and equality" as a principle of social relations becomes, in Marxism, entirely conditional upon elements borrowed from the capitalist system, culture, and Western morals, to wit: (1) mechanism, (2) techno-bureaucracy, (3) acquisitiveness, (4) economic competition, and (5) the individual profit motive? At last, the ultimate goal comes into sight: the greatest possible degree of material prosperity.

The question naturally arises, So what is the fundamental difference in philosophy of life between Marxism and the bourgeoisie? After all, the difference between the two theses "Capital will be at the disposal of a single class" and "Capital will be at the disposal of the state" is the difference between two systems, not that between two philosophies or two different conceptions of life, humanity, moral values, or the universe.

Accordingly, if we infer that, from the standpoint of outlook as well, Marxism shares the bourgeois world-view, anthropology, and morals, and that inasmuch as it appeared in a Western bourgeois cultural setting (the inevitable product of the infrastructure of its age), it shares the intellectual content, spirit, and object in life of its adversary the bourgeoisie, have we judged it unfairly?

Not at all! As Marx fully accepts, the Western bourgeoisie comprises not merely an economic system, but likewise a particular spirit, outlook, anthropology, philosophy of life, and morality. Through these, in which all spiritual motives are dismissed in favor of the dominion of base material life over all the higher qualities of humanity, it addresses man as a being who will work, deceive, and wage war all the more in order to eat all the more.

Therefore, as Professor Grimbert says, "Isn't it true that Marxism is trying its utmost to build a totally *embourgeoise* society?" That is to say, the difference between Marxism and the Western bourgeoisie lies in the fact that one promotes a bourgeois *class,* and the other a bourgeois *society.*

Saint-Simon, founder of the "religion of industrialism," divides society into two classes: the industrial class, which has a role in production and is composed of workers, engineers, capitalists, and factory workers; and the class of parasites, composed of consumers uninvolved in production, such as intellectuals, writers, artists, clergy, philosophers, heroes, statesmen, athletes, soldiers, and so forth. This outlook, exemplifying the utmost in worship of production and even placing worker and capitalist in a single class (one disposed against the spiritual and cultural forces of society, at that), despite its apparent opposition to the outlook of Marx from the standpoint of sociology, resembles it in the essence of its philosophy, its approach to man.

In Communist China, we know, the very small steel blast furnaces set up in the villages have come to be regarded as symbols of the revolution and designated "the People's Sacred Blast Furnaces." In the Soviet Union, a major author has written a book entitled *The Cult of Cement;* prompted by this mentality, it maintains that responsibility for human civilization, culture, and well-being has been transferred from God, morals, philosophy, science, and so forth—to cement!

At this point, it is appropriate to relate the opinion of one of the most outstanding and dedicated Marxist intellectuals of Lenin's and even Engels' time [i.e., Edouard Berth]. In his work *Les Nouveaux Aspects du socialisme,* in a remarkable phrase, he says quite seriously, "Marxism is the philosophy of the producers." (If this be true, given actual experience, facts, and figures, American capitalism has every right to claim superiority to Marxism.)

THE CENTRAL PROBLEM, however, appears to remain insoluble: how does this humanism or primacy of man, oft-cited and much vaunted by Marx as he does battle with the bourgeoisie, result from the primacy of production?

Taking as our starting point the universal human ideals, we see how, the closer we draw to the letter and spirit of Marxism, the farther we are from the spirit of Islam. The two ways diverge.

Islam, very simply, is a philosophy of human liberation. Its first summons, "Say 'There is no god but God' and prosper," propounds *tauhid* as the necessary means to that end.

We see that from the same beginning, Islamic humanism ascends to a kind of awareness, while Marxist humanism proceeds to a kind of production. Then does Islam lead to a mystical and ascetic idealism foreign to actuality? Has Islam, like the mystical religions and ideologies, forgotten the principle of justice? Not at all! Islam addresses economic welfare and social justice as principles of its social order; indeed it stresses them. To be precise, in Islam these principles constitute essential prerequisites; they can free man from poverty and discrimination so that, through moral growth and particular evolution, he may freely unfold his inherent divine nature. This is paramount to the philosophy of human life in Islam.

Islam and Marxism also differ in their basic criteria for interpreting human moral values or humanism.

Here we must point to what is at the same time one of the most glaring and one of the least noted of Marxism's self-contradictions, one that is simultaneously the major factor in its success in attracting minds and hearts and the major factor in its failure to realize its own proclaimed ideals. For, to be brief, Marxism has emerged as a major source of opposition to Marxism.

Many intellectuals who have been made painfully aware of this contradiction, without fully resolving or even quite admitting it, have followed the line of least resistance in accounting for it; they have posited an essential difference between Marxism as a school and the existing Marxist regimes, distinguished subjective Marxism from objective Marxism, and regarded the Marxist regimes as having strayed from the principles of Marxism (for which reason those regimes have not achieved the original aims of Marxism as its founders envisioned them). Then these intellectuals have sought to resolve the contradiction in their own minds by exchanging such accusations and curses as "Revisionism!" "Personality cult!" "Nationalism!" "*Embourgeoisement!*" "Collaboration!" "Titoism!" "Stalinism!" "Maoism!" and so forth.

In truth, the contradiction lies in the very sources of the ideology. It is a contradiction between ends and means—the contradiction between man in Marxist philosophy and man in Marxist society!

When Marx speaks of man, and in particular when he speaks with fervor and profundity of the infamy of capitalism, bourgeois culture and social organization, and Western industry, and of the waste of human potential in that system—when he rises to the defense of human freedom—he assumes such a mystical tone that one would suppose him a visionary, a Platonist philosopher, a moralist, or even a man of the cloth. In condemning the capitalist system based on private property, workmen's wages, the value of money, the principle of competition, and so forth, Marx relies for the most part on the conception that the reality of man as a sublime essence has been defiled and constricted by this system, and that ignoble values have been substituted for human values. Even as Marx discusses his own materialism in relation to humanity, the tone he adopts recalls the moralists. Where he wishes to demonstrate the reasons why materialism must be the basis of communism, he ascribes to materialism attributes that are altogether the province of religion, or at any rate that of moral philosophy. He gives an idealistic cast to Marxist sociology: "It does not require a great deal of insight to see that materialism, owing to its views of intrinsic goodness, the equal gifts of intelligence among all people, the sublime capacity for experience, familiarization, and learning, the equal rights of people to pleasure and the like, is necessarily connected to communism and socialism."

Where, in defense of humanity and praise of the proletariat, he attacks Christianity, he assumes the tone of a Christian and employs words commonly used in works on religious morality or moral idealism: "The social principles of Christianity preach dishonor, contemptibility, abjectness, servility, humility, in short all ignoble qualities. The proletariat, refusing to accept this debasement, has much greater need of courage, self-respect, pride, and the desire for independence than of bread." Is this Marx speaking about the proletariat, or is it Jean Jacques Rousseau, or maybe Ernest Renan or John Stuart Mill?

When he speaks of man's alienation from himself, Marx is a spiritual humanist praising the true, independent, sacred essence of humanity as the original source of virtuous qualities and a transcendental and free nature, nobler than all other creatures: "The more the worker devotes himself to his work and the stronger the alien world created by him becomes, the more impoverished he becomes in his individual self, his inner world. This holds equally true of religion: the more humanity gives itself up to God, the less it belongs to itself." Here we see very plainly that Marx, in discussing humanity, accepts an inner world and an outer world, a self and an environment. (It is especially interesting that he sees an inverse relation between them!) One feels clearly that he is defending here an "independent" humanism, in his own words a "self-subsisting human nature," in the face of God, society, and nature. As Marx attacks religion, he raises man still higher in spirituality, as if he were a holy being, the Creator Himself, while God, meaning the manifestation of all sacred and absolute moral values, is the reflection of man's holy and transcendental essence.

In all the works he and Engels have written on the subject of man, they speak of him as a reality replete with "virtuous qualities" and "sublime eternal values." He is free, thinking, capable of choice, an "independent cause" superior to material causation in nature, history, and society. He is distinguished by a sense of honor, by courage, creativity, philanthropy, a readiness to sacrifice himself for his beliefs, and a sense of responsibility toward others. Finally, he is the maker of his own destiny and intrinsic nature, and even "prophet" and "savior" to his own people.

This is Marx the philosopher speaking about man, Marx who has constructed his humanism from elements derived directly or indirectly from religion, mysticism, moral philosophy, and particularly from seventeenth-century humanism and early nineteenth-century German moral socialism. Thus Andre Piettre, among many, has spoken in all seriousness of a "mystic" or "spiritual man" in this humanism of Marx's. This is no exaggeration; one may succinctly describe this man Marx is eulogizing as a two-legged god roaming the earth.

However, as soon as Marx the philosopher falls silent, Marx the sociologist undoes all he has accomplished. He takes this being who was seated on the divine throne and hurls him headlong to the ground. This mighty creator who has created God, history, and even himself, and who has transformed nature to conform to his self-aware and dominating will, suddenly turns out to have been created by his own economic tools, themselves the inevitable product of the law of dialectical materialism. Those tools fabricate two things: goods and man.

Swiftly, Marx the sociologist transforms the nature of the "man become God" of Marx the philosopher into one befitting "man become goods." He speaks of the human constitution in terms that would have enraged or at least alarmed his alter ego: "For socialist man, everything in all of human history except the natural human form is the product of work." Engels, in his essay "The Role of Work in Humanizing the Ape," adds:

> Economists call work the origin of all wealth, but work is infinitely more than that: work is the essential condition for all human life, such that, from one point of view, work has created man himself, ... in truth, work has turned ape into man.... The kind of tools with which man works determines the mode of work, which is the infrastructure, in accordance with the character of which the social system, the kind of ownership, the legal system, government, religion, philosophy, literature, arts, moral values, ideology, and culture take shape, the shape they take always being conformable to that infrastructure, or rather being its product.

Then, we should ask, is humanity anything other than the aggregate of those ideological, cultural, and moral values which in turn are the superstructure and the product of the mode of work?

Most importantly and most frighteningly, sociological Marxism propounds the concepts of capitalism, exploitation, class contradictions, and private and social ownership in a manner fundamentally different from that of philosophical Marxism. (In the view of Marx the sociologist, capitalism is under no circumstances to be condemned as inhuman, but only as being impossible today.)

Please consider closely the following remarks and note the roles played by humanity, thought, responsibility, moral values, and in particular the high value accorded such ideals as justice, the elimination of slavery, and the realization of socialism:

> Human beings, in the social production of their lives, enter a necessary and predetermined stage which is independent of their will.
>
> ********
>
> These production relationships are in accordance with a specific degree of development and deployment of the forces of material production. The aggregate of these relationships constitutes the economic structure of a society, that is, the actual foundation upon

which is constructed a legal and political superstructure conforming to specific forms of social consciousness.

****

In material life, the mode of production determines the flow of social, political, and intellectual life. It is not human consciousness that determines human existence; on the contrary, it is man's social existence that determines his consciousness.

****

Social relations generally are connected with the forces of production. The hand mill exemplifies feudal society, and the steam engine exemplifies the society of industrial capitalism.

So it is that the means of production (the hand mill, spinning wheel, shovel, hammer and anvil, steam engine, or huge assemblages of industrial machinery) inevitably gives shape to the mode of production, which in turn generates the social superstructure. That is, the infrastructure through economic necessity creates certain legal, social, moral, and cultural forms, and certain class relations. Part of this superstructure is ownership.

In earlier times, when the mode of production was manual labor, and individual, it accorded with a superstructure of private ownership. The machine, however, transformed the mode of production, making it collective. Accordingly, the infrastructure became collective, while the superstructure continued to be one of individual ownership and thus in contradiction with it.

That is why industrial capitalism is confronted with contradictions between the productive infrastructure, which has become collective, and the superstructure of ownership, which attempts to preserve the order of the individual. This lack of homogeneity necessarily culminates in revolution, in that the productive infrastructure seeks a superstructure in conformity with itself—collective ownership; socialism is nothing other than the realization of a superstructure that is congruent with the infrastructure of mechanism.

Is it not possible to deduce from this precise analysis a justification for all the social systems, class relations, religious and ethical norms and tendencies, and judicial and legal forms of the pre-industrial age? As the texts of Marxism make clear, in the dialectical materialist theory of history, even the causes of slavery may be deduced from this rule: slavery too is the particular social superstructure of the agricultural mode of production. That is, as primitive communal society changed its mode of production from hunting to agriculture, there arose a need to recruit new forces for production. This historical necessity caused the recruitment of animals (domestication) and the recruitment of human beings (slavery) to come into practice. Accordingly, in every social order and every historical period, the existing conditions have taken the specific form appropriate to the mode of production, that mode itself being determined by the form of the existing tools.

In this Marxist sociology and philosophy of history, we see the fearful grave that Marx the sociologist and economist has dug for the "man become god" created by Marx the philosopher and anthropologist. Now we are in a better position to understand that remark of Edouard Berth, the well-known Marxist, that Marxism essentially is the philosophy of the producers.

Given a logic that analyzes human history, society, life, culture, thought, and ideals in this manner, what does it mean to say that the capitalist order leads to the corruption of morals and values, of humanism and the essence of man? For as long as Marx does his best in his analysis of society and history to keep his sociology faithful to the barren "scientific" outlook and the cramped consensus of "existing realities" (assuming that he has done so, which is highly questionable), how can his words be other than empty when he speaks of truth, value, oppression and justice, freedom or slavery during the ages of manual labor and agriculture?

On the basis of this outlook, we not only would have to call all the sociologists before Marx utopians, but also would have to say that all those who have fought for justice—the saviors and leaders, the masses who struggled against slavery, feudalism, exploitation, the oppressive systems of private property, and even against superstitious and stagnant religions, cultures, and customs—essentially struggled in vain. For because they were unaware of the determining character of the mode of production in their time, they were daydreaming and became utopians. Had they only been versed in the materialist philosophy of history and in scientific socialism, of course they would have accepted the social contexts and legal norms of their times, as well as private ownership and its style of interpersonal relations, however inhuman, because those relations conformed to the economic infrastructure. They would have waited patiently for the appearance of the promised messiah, the machine, which would collectivize labor. Then, through a dialectical miracle, the paradise promised by the religions would be realized within industrial capitalist society, and man would live there as a contented god.

But what values would this contented machine-made god hold? What moral virtues? How would he remedy the corrupt morals engendered by the bourgeois order? And what is the meaning of "corrupt morals," given that every morality is part of a superstructure over something determined by the mode of production? What moral criteria exist? Indeed, Lenin, the practical exponent and architect of Marxism, who actually experienced the concrete reality of Marxism at closer hand than Marx himself, discarded the "mystical" humanism Marx had counterposed to bourgeois reality and officially proclaimed: "For us, moral principles have no existence apart from society. Such principles are lies" (On Religion).

It is clear why Islam views this low and cold-hearted representation of man, morals, and history with such loathing!

Why should Marxism acknowledge a set of divine values for man and quickly move to deprive him of them? Why should it, in its philosophy of history, call this god-unto-himself a boulder standing in the way of the coursing river of dialectical materialism, and, in its sociology, consider him a piece of merchandise to be altered through the means of production, and then finally, in an actual socialist order, treat him like a component installed in a totally organized and programmed social structure?

Such a drastic decline within the Marxist order is an unavoidable fate for Marxist man. That is because the moral values and nobility of human nature that Marx ascribes to humanity have no logical and scientific basis; he must of necessity seek their origin in one of two sources. He may look to physical nature, there to come up against the naturalism of his day, where man is a static being among animals and objects; but he disavows this position heatedly. He may see man's origins in matter: he may stoop to the materialism prevalent in his own time, what he terms "vulgar materialism," and embrace the vision of a clockwork universe; but this too he refutes.

Marx and, later, Engels proclaim, in an effort to free humanity from the anti-human constraints of base naturalism and "vulgar" materialism, that with the discovery of "dialectics" and its adjunction to "materialism" they avoid all the unfortunate consequences of materialism—because dialectics considers humanity neither a material object nor a natural being, static and lifeless, but a reality in the process of "becoming," by means of its own efforts and through a process of contradiction and conflict.

If Hegel maintains such a superiority for his dialectic, his words merit consideration because he regards man as the ultimate synthesis of the "absolute idea of Being" and its antithesis, the material world. Accordingly, in relation to nature and matter, man in Hegelianism is a first cause and noble element.

But Marx has, in his own words, "overturned" this principle. By giving matter precedence over idea (pronouncing idea a thing proceeding inexorably toward man from the heart of matter), he denies man as an aware, thinking, and willing self. Concerning what he has done to the Hegelian dialectic and humanism, he explains, "Since Hegel's man walked on his head, this overturning enables him to stand now and walk on his two feet" (to which a Muslim writer has retorted, "Isn't man really a being who walks on his head?").

Marx invokes the ancient Greek philosopher Heraclitus, who says, "One cannot enter the same river more than once" (which is to say, everything is in flux), in support of his dialectical materialism. But if Marx has "overturned" the Hegelian dialectic, he has altogether undone that of Heraclitus.

The Greek philosopher, although considering everything as undergoing transformation, clearly propounds the existence of two constant principles: a sublime substance, which he terms "fire," and a constant logical order, which he calls *logos.* This dialectics has no resemblance whatever to Marx's completely materialistic dialectics in which, as Lenin says, the only principle of existence is change. On the contrary, it is closely allied with the mystical conception of opposites in the Eastern religions, especially as it is found in Zoroastrianism, Manicheanism, Judaism, Christianity, Islam, and Sufism. That is because, in this conception, although man and the universe are grounded in the strife of opposites (good and evil, Ahura Mazda and Ahriman, light and darkness, man and Iblis), two constant principles likewise exist: one, the movement of the cosmos toward perfection, and the other, the sacred essence or eternal spirit that rules over the cosmos.

Marx, however, having denied the existence of these two principles and accepting only absolute mutability based on contradiction, is of course unable to maintain a position that turns on humanism or eternal human moral values, since nothing that can be relied upon exists in this "passing river." Thus it is only natural that those concepts of human nature and moral values that Marx employed in defending humanism emerge in the context of Marxist society as mutable, capricious material attributes that appear and disappear in accordance with the exigencies of a given system of production, and that no principle should remain. As Lenin says, "All moral principles are lies."

Islam, on the other hand, in maintaining that the divine element in humanity (as opposed to the principle of Iblis) originates in something superior to material nature, matter, the productive infrastructure of society, and so forth, is able to speak of constant and primal moral values, of a good, indeed holy primordial nature, and of the progressive and creative qualities of mankind.

Marx says goodness is innate in man, but, in the first place, what is goodness in a materialistic cosmos? And in the second place, in this sweeping flow in which all is subject to transformation, to speak of an unchanging disposition is altogether anti-dialectical.

Islam, while speaking of all things (in accordance with the scientific experience of nature) as loci of generation and decay, believes there is an aspect of being that is constant and evolutionary, so that whatever is aligned with it remains in the universe eternally: *"Everything is perishing except that which is oriented toward Him"* (28:88).

Islam makes not a single unscientific or unrealistic assessment of humanity; it views it as arising from dust (matter), but maintains that it bears an aptitude not of dust, designated as the primordial nature, which is a reflection of the absolute universal Will, that is, of God. (*"This is the primordial nature of mankind, in which God has created it"* [30:40].)

Thus humanity is a twofold essence, intermediate between nature and God, pursuing its evolutionary movement from dust to God according to its own choice. It is in this context that the terms responsibility and innate goodness may be applied to it. It is also in this context that one may speak of a true and logical humanism, a humanism that neither falls into the pit of materialism nor becomes a toy in an unconscious, involuntary game of dialectics. It likewise does not assume the form of a metaphysical abstraction cut off from reality, nature, and society.

It is in this way that Islam, in contrast with Marxism, is in a position to defend the principles termed justice, nobility, guidance, awareness, responsibility, moral values, and human virtues, which are known to every system throughout human history, and it is for this reason that Islam does not have to wait for the appearance of a steam engine to realize them!

———

THE IDEOLOGIES—ancient and modern—that today summon people to themselves fall in general into the categories of mystical religions (Christianity and the Eastern religions, especially Buddhism and Hinduism), materialism (in its various forms), Western liberalism, nihilism, existentialism, and Marxism.

Other than Marxism, all of them, religious or not, are partial, one-dimensional ideologies, and it is only Islam that is able to confront each within its particular dimension. Islam has a purely religious confrontation with Christianity and the Eastern mystical religions, a philosophical opposition to materialism, and an anthropological, and hence moral, dispute with existentialism. It collides with liberalism over social and economic issues. There would be no point in trying to relate it to nihilism, for nihilism abandons everything.

Of them all only Marxism has constructed a complete, multifaceted ideology, and Islam, as a religion and as a people [ummah], conflicts with it in every dimension. Marxism, among all the new ideologies, is unique in that it struggles to base every aspect of human life—material and spiritual, philosophical and practical, individual and social—upon its peculiar materialistic world-view. It is for this reason that the system afflicts every dimension of human life with the calamity of materialism. Islam, alone among all the historical religions, has this same comprehensiveness. It does not confine itself to ordering the relations between man and God, or to the purification of the soul (as do Christianity and Buddhism); it presents itself as a school comprehending the various aspects of human life, ranging from philosophic outlook to individual daily life. Thus these two schools stand before men and invite them to one of two opposed intellectual bases and world-views.

Neither of the two is susceptible to division. In the first place, all the elements and dimensions of each have coalesced along the lines of its distinctive world outlook, diametrically opposed to the other; to add any element or dimension to either, or to take one away, could only result in the collapse of the whole structure. Secondly, an ideology is an interrelated whole with a single spirit and essence, and a unique *raison d'etre*. To try to resolve it into its constituent elements would be like killing it and then dissecting the corpse.

That is why these two ideologies, as two fully developed systems, stand opposed in every respect, and that is why, as

Henry Martinet concluded, "Marxism, in spite of the favorable political and economic conditions that have cropped up at various times in the last hundred years, has achieved successes in none of the Islamic societies (in contrast with the Far East and Latin America). One must look for the cause solely in Islam." Why? Because, unlike Christianity and Buddhism, Islam resists Marxism not in the philosophical dimension alone, but in every dimension and aspect, because it has its own claims in them.

Since Marxism is founded on materialism and considers man's essential origin to be dust, its humanism ends up reducing man to the status of an object.

Since Islam bases its divine humanism on *tauhid*, on the scientific level it defines man as of the earth, while on the level of existential analysis it raises him from dust toward God and absolute transcendental values.

Since Marxism accounts human values as relative phenomena relating to the societal superstructure, based on the mode of production, it lets them all lapse to the level of material expediency.

Since it accounts values to be the emanations of divine attributes in the human sphere, Islam, although it holds economics to be a genuine concern, is able to superimpose on it this system of values and to distinguish principle from ideal. Since it holds that man reflects the existential dualism of dust/God, it is in a position to account for the dualism of profit and value (or economy and morals) in human life, without having to deny one for the sake of the other, as do the mystical religions and Marxism.

Marxism, by conjoining the Hegelian dialectic and materialism and also by introducing the concept of the tools of material production, arrives at a materialistic determinism bound up with the same tools of production, which completely undermines the conception of man as will and consequently leaves the principle of human responsibility without justification.

Islam grants that society possesses ordering principles and that the continuous evolutionary movement of human history is based upon scientific laws. But because it considers the human will to be a manifestation of the universal Will of Being (and not an unwitting product of the exigencies of production or of society), Islam never hurls it into the terrible pit of materialistic determinism. Likewise, by proclaiming the principle of assignation or "descent" [hobut], it frees mankind from the bond of divine determinism in which the Eastern religions are caught.

Marxism, when it wishes to deny religion, calls God an outward manifestation of the human essence, setting man in God's place in the universe. But when it wishes to demonstrate historical materialism, it makes this man, the creator of God, the product of the tools of production!

Islam situates humanity in a world of *tauhid*, where God, man, and nature display a meaningful and purposeful harmony. It presents Adam as the principial essence of the species humanity, as dust into which God has breathed His spirit, as intermediate between spirit and matter. Further, it places the divine trust exclusively in his hands; in this way it presents a basis beyond that of matter for the principle of human responsibility. Through the parable of Eve and Iblis, with its concept of rebellion, Islam situates the principles of *eros* and *logos* in man's essence and formalizes the independence of the human will from divine predestination. Through the principle of descent (from heaven to earth), it dispatches him into earthly life, so that he may realize heaven through his will, love, awareness, and responsibility, amid contradiction and suffering, and so that he may forge his ultimate destiny with his own two hands. The Resurrection is *"the Day on which man will see what his two hands have sent forward"* (79:40).

Since worship, when conscious and heartfelt, becomes a manifestation of all absolute sacred values, the worshipper nourishes these values in a relative human mode in his own being. Thus he sustains his essential being in a state of sincerity, refines his feelings, grows steadfast in his pursuit of essential perfection, and gains a sense of detachment from "dust" (objective material existence). By basing his existence upon *tauhid* (as a world-view and a moral philosophy, and likewise as both a way of life and life's essential and ultimate meaning), he achieves deliverance.[5]

The opposing ways in which Islam and Marxism approach humanity may be summed up in several pairs of examples:

1. Marxism, because it is founded on an absolutely materialistic world-view, is incapable of raising humanity in its essence, attributes, or evolutionary state beyond the narrow confines of materiality; it necessarily ranks it along with all other beings in the confines of an unconscious and purposeless nature.

Islam, in holding to the world-view of *tauhid*, is able to justify man as a divine essence, grant him transcendental attributes, extend his evolution to the infinite, and thus situate humanity in a living, meaningful, and infinite universe whose dimensions extend far beyond what even the sciences can represent.

2. Marxism, in accepting only the conception of matter of classical physics, is forced through materialistic analysis to retract all it has said about the essential glory and noble primacy of humanity. Thus the glorious being envisioned by Marx the philosopher and humanist—the creator of God—is suddenly reduced to a piece of merchandise, a product of the tools employed in crafts, agriculture, or industry.

Islam, in explaining the world of matter and the primordial nature of man as two signs of one exalted Being and absolute Consciousness, is able simultaneously to accept the existence of a reciprocal impact of man upon environment and environment upon man, and also, insofar as man acts as a cause in the chain of causality, to uphold the human station without reference to natural and social determinations. It guards humanity from slipping into the pit of materialist, historicist, or sociologist fanaticism, so that the primacy of man will not be transformed into a primacy of matter or of tools.

[5] It is for this reason that the Messenger of Islam began his mission with only the declaration of *tauhid,* and confined himself to repeating it for three years, while specifying the ultimate intent of *tauhid* to be human deliverance: *"Say, 'La ilaha illa 'llah [There is no god but God],' and be delivered."*

3. Marxism, remaining fiercely loyal to materialist realism, relinquishes its right to speak of values or to make judgements on the basis of them.

Islam, maintaining a belief in an absolute source for values beyond the empirical realm, can justify them logically.

4. Marxism, because it considers man to be the product of his social environment, which in turn is an aggregate of shifting structures and circumstances, is unable to base itself on a constant principle such as the human essence or human reality. Having denied both God and the primordial nature of man, it has relinquished the authentic basis for the human values that make up the body of morals. Consequently, as Lenin puts it, "All talk of moral principles is a lie."

Just as Islam maintains the existence of constant principles in nature upon which science is based, it asserts that constant principles exist in our primordial nature and form the basis of morals. According to Islam, human values are just as authentic and demonstrable as natural laws. Contrary to Marxism, which tries to equate those values with social customs and to bury them in the depths of an economic and social materialism, Islam is totally committed to freeing them from the mutable yet coercive conditions and exigencies of material life by rooting them in the primordial nature of man and showing them to be reflections of the Absolute shining upon the human conscience.

5. Marxism, by annexing "dialectical" to "materialism" in order to arrive at an explanation for historical and social change, has arrived at a materialistic determinism in which man has given up his primacy and become the plaything of this blind process of contradiction. Consequently, it denies whatever it has claimed by way of humanism and completely deprives humanity of all freedom and responsibility.

Islam, seeing this element of contradiction in the human constitution, does not deny freedom (choice) or its consequence, responsibility, but sees them as issuing from precisely this contradiction. It defines man as a being in contradiction, having the dual essence of clay and divine spirit, and as a will that can choose either one over the other. His human responsibility urges him to place his earthly half at the service of his divine half for the sake of its growth, and thus to achieve existential clarity and purity of spirit. In this way he may transmute his existential dichotomy to *tauhid* and assume divine characteristics.

We see that through the annexation of Marxist dialectics to materialism, a materialistic determinism is produced that logically denies human choice and its consequence, human responsibility: human choice is seen as arising from dialectics, while responsibility arises from choice.

6. Marxism has "overturned" the Hegelian dialectic, changing it from one based on idealism to one based on realism. But this has ruined the dialectics of Heraclitus, since Heraclitus, although he envisions everything as in perpetual movement and change, maintains two constant principles alongside this change: one, fire and the other, *logos*. This shows that the true outlook of dialectics (as opposed to the one popularized by Marx) has been a mystical one from the start. Substantiating this fact are Western philosophies from that of Heraclitus in ancient Greece to that of Hegel in the nineteenth century, as well as the world-views of all the great Eastern religions: Zoroastrianism, the Taoism of Lao Tzu, Manicheanism, Hinduism, Buddhism, and the Abrahamic religions (Judaism, Christianity, and Islam). All these explain the world according to the principle of contradiction and change (i.e., generation and decay).

Heraclitus exemplifies a typically mystical world-view in his use of fire to symbolize the sacred and eternal substance, and *logos* to symbolize the constant order and harmony of a universe in total transformation. Marxism, by denying these two constant principles in dialectics, has denied any constant aspect or eternal order in the universe or in humanity. Thus its humanism is expressed not as a flow, but as a succession of waves, amidst which there is nothing to cling to.

7. In the words of Berth, "Marxism is the philosophy of the producers."

In the language of the Qur'an, Islam is the philosophy of guidance.

8. Marxism supposes that man has created God. Man whom it has thus raised to the empyrean finds there no throne to occupy; the tether of an overturned and defective dialectics inevitably drags him immediately to the ground, where he is handed over to the tools of production and the mode of production, and condemned to suffer a historical determinism.

Islam regards man as having a non-material nature. Maintaining that God has created man, it renders him independent of natural and material determinations. In speaking of man's fateful rebellion in paradise, it presents him as a will independent from that of his Creator, thus freeing him from the ties of divine predestination. In this way, by presenting man as an aware being possessed of a will and freed from the captivity of heaven and earth alike, it arrives at true humanism. Then it has man accorded the unique trust that all the world had balked at but man accepted, which causes all the angels (symbolizing all the forces of the universe) to prostrate themselves at his feet. Finally, Islam looks upon him as God's vice-regent in nature and has him sent forth into this world, so that, like some nature god, he may subjugate the world and build his own destiny through self-awareness, amid contradiction and suffering. Thus he may return to God self-aware.

We see how very far such a philosophy's approach to humanity and humanism is from that of the "philosophy of the producers."

The great contemporary student of Islam, Iqbal, has had the last word on this point: "Islam and communism both talk about man and summon man to themselves; but communism has taken pains to draw man from God to dust, while Islam, on the contrary, is striving to raise him up from the dust to God."

We see clearly that Islam and Marxism are moving in opposite directions on the road of humanism, with the consequence that either one may be affirmed only by denying the other.

Those persons in particular who see Islam as the only path leading through the modern calamities to true deliverance for humanity should carefully consider the words of Andre

Piettre, the contemporary student of Marxism, as he uncovers its true face:

> Marx's school of thought is in truth indivisible; it presents itself as an all-embracing perspective on man and the universe; such is its alphabet.
> Thus, this school takes precisely the place of the religions and wars against them fiercely.

One might conclude the same for Islam in relation to all of the ideologies that address man and the universe.

NOW OUR CONCLUSION is coming into view. Humanism, which all post-Renaissance humanitarian intellectuals hoped would take over the task of human liberation from religion, has become a sacred article of faith for all the atheistic schools of recent centuries. However, it loses its sacrosanct aura as soon as it is subjected to logical scrutiny and proves an idle speculation, which, like some literary expression, bespeaks utopian values or Platonic wisdoms that are sublime and beautiful but have no application in the real world.

True humanism is a collection of the divine values in man that constitute his morals and religious cultural heritage. Modern ideologies, in denying religion, are unable to account for these values. Consequently, although calling themselves staunchly realist, they become more idealistic than Plato, even as they entangle humanity still further in their fanatical materialism.

Poor man—always searching for deliverance and finding only disaster. In his flight from the oppression of the powerful and the slave-masters, he turned to the great religions and followed the prophets, and so endured struggles and martyrdoms only to be captured by the Magi, Caliphs, Brahmans, and, most terrible of all, the dark and deadly tumult of the Medieval Church, in the midst of which the Pope, as representative of the celestial God, ruled the earth like some imperious

Jehovah, holding the reins of politics, property, and faith, and making servants of intellect and science.

Generations struggled and sacrificed to bring about a Renaissance, to mobilize humanity to pursue science and liberation, so that it might be freed from what had been inflicted upon it in the name of religion.

Humanity arrived at liberalism, and took democracy in place of theocracy as its key to liberation. It was snared by a crude capitalism, in which democracy proved as much a delusion as theocracy. Liberalism proved an arena in which the only freedom was for horsemen, vying with one another in raids and plundering. Again humanity became the hapless victim sacrificed to the unchecked powers that brought science, technique, and everyday life into orbit around their maddening and continually growing greed and search for profits.

The desire for equality, for liberation from this dizzying whirl of personal avarice, so horrifyingly accelerated by the machine, led humanity into a revolt that resulted in communism. This communism, however, simply represents the same fanatical and frightening power as the Medieval Church, only without God. It has its popes, but they rule not in the name of the Lord but in the name of the proletariat. These absolute despots and "sole proprietors" also claim quasi-prophetic and -spiritual honors and pontificate on matters of science, belief, morals, art, and literature.

As the communist system, in the name of justice, comes to dominate those peoples who have fled the oppression and exploitation of Western capitalism, the sentiment of an old, freedom-loving Muslim poet is echoed:

> O, would that the oppression of the sons of Marwan
>   were returned to us,
> And the justice of the sons of Abbas consumed in
>   the flames!

But the spirit never dies. I am referring to the spirit that the Qur'an speaks of: not the individual soul, but the divine life-giving and animating power that, like Seraphiel's trumpet, sounds over the skeletal forms of the ages, so that they rise up from those deathly silent graves dug for the human spirit, which so longs for deliverance. Then—a fresh ferment, a new resurrection begins, and humanity faces life anew in a new age.

Now that this spirit has been breathed into the corpse of this century, during which mankind reached an existential dead end, this humanity which has suffered so greatly in its search for liberation, having undergone bitter experiences with Western capitalism and struck its head against the blank wall of communism, seeks a third road between this one to the tavern and that to the temple, a third road which it is the mission of the Third World to set out upon.

What makes this future stand out in greater and more promising relief is the fact that in the capitalist and Marxist worlds alike, powerful spirits have come to self-awareness and raised their heads above the tumult and din of capitalist mechanism to decry the disastrous deformation of a humanity that, trapped in an aimless liberalism with a fake veneer of democracy, is becoming one-dimensional, impoverished, and alienated from itself and is losing its human identity.

Here, in the very teeth of the forces that have all the dimensions of society in their grasp, this spirit has called out. Its call reaches the ears of the age across the high and massive walls that have been thrown up around it, reaching further and penetrating deeper day by day. It is still too soon to depict the future that is in the making, but we may foresee its general direction.

What all the new appeals have in common is a belief that both the roads onto which Western capitalism and communism have driven humanity culminate in a human disaster, that the way to human liberation therefore consists in turning away from both of them.

Apart from this shared negative view, however, one may discern a positive one in all those appeals and searches: a quest for the spirit.

We might be too optimistic if we were to interpret all this as a turning to religion, but we may speak with assurance of an aspiring spiritual tendency. There is implicit and even explicit in the words of most of the intellectuals who decry the human disaster taking place in both these (outwardly) conflicting worlds a revulsion against the materialism of today's philosophy and morals, against the distortion of the true essence of man and the loss of transcendental human values. One mourns the loss of "that Ahuran sun" that shone out from the depths of human nature, clarifying man's existence, illuminating his life, infusing spirit into the natural world, and creating love and values.

Today, in philosophy, Heidegger does not speak in the terms of Hegel or Feuerbach. In science, Max Planck, the outstanding exponent of the new physics, opposes the ideas of Claude Bernard. Heidegger is searching for Christ in humanity, and Planck is searching for God in the world of physics. Modern literature and art, expressing alarm at the futility of modern life, review the deformation of modern man and the dark and deadly loneliness that has enveloped him. Eliot, Strindberg, Guenon, Pasternak, Toynbee, Erich Fromm, Senghor, Uzghan, Omar Mawlud—all are in some way searching for light. Even a well-known contemporary physiologist, Alexis Carrel (winner of two Nobel prizes for his work in grafting blood vessels and in preserving living tissues outside the body), speaks unself-consciously about "grace" as a powerful factor in the moral and psychological development and harmonious growth of a person.

It even appears that a sort of messianic spirit has sprung up in the closed fortress of the communist world, and a human renaissance is taking place. This is occurring despite intensified state opposition to religion, zealous efforts by the ruling party to pacify the new generation of artists and intellectuals and bring them into line with dialectical materialist dogma, and the intimidating exercises of the apparatus of thought control to suppress "reactionary" ideas, "bourgeois" tendencies, and religious activity.

Today, in contrast to Marx, who felt human liberation depended upon the denial of God, and Nietzsche, who boasted, "God is dead," even an atheistic philosopher like Sartre speaks of God's absence from the universe "with painful regret," seeing in this a source of the futility of man and existence, the loss of values.

Thirty years ago Iqbal proclaimed, "Today, more than anything else, humanity needs a spiritual interpretation of the universe." Although it is implicit in Iqbal's words, we might add, "It needs a spiritual interpretation of humanity as well." We are clearly standing on the frontier between two eras— one where both Western civilization and communist ideology have failed to liberate humanity, drawing it instead into disaster and causing the new spirit to recoil in disillusionment; and one where humanity in search of deliverance will try a new road and take a new direction, and will liberate its essential nature. Over this dark and dispirited world, it will set a holy lamp like a new sun; by its light, the man alienated from himself will perceive anew his primordial nature, rediscover himself, and see clearly the path of salvation.

Islam will play a major role in this new life and movement. In the first place, with its pure *tauhid*, it offers a profound spiritual interpretation of the universe, one that is as noble and idealistic as it is logical and intelligible. In the second place, through the philosophy of the creation of Adam, Islam reveals in its humanism the conception of a free, independent, noble essence, but one that is as fully attuned to earthly reality as it is divine and idealistic.

This is especially true from this standpoint: Islam does not content itself with answering only one philosophical or spiritual need, or with presenting only one ethical viewpoint; it strives to realize the world-view of *tauhid* and of human primacy within real life. Unlike the subjectivist philosophies and mystical religions, it does not accept in human existence the dichotomies of sacred and profane, belief and behavior, idea and actuality. Thus Louis Gardet says, "Islam is both a religion and a nation."

This future, which begins with the discarding of capitalism and Marxism, is neither predestined nor prefabricated. Instead, it remains to be built. There is no doubt that Islam will have an appropriate role in its construction, when it has freed itself from the effects of centuries of stagnation, superstition, and contamination, and is put forth as a living ideology.

That is the task of the true intellectuals of Islam. Only in this way will Islam—after a renaissance of belief and an emergence from isolation and reaction—be able to take part in the current war of beliefs and, in particular, to command the center and serve as an example to contemporary thought, where the new human spirit is seeking the means to begin a new world and a new humanity.

This is no extravagant proposal; it is a duty. Not only does the essential summons of Islam require it, but the text of the Qur'an explicitly enjoins it upon the true followers of Islam: *"God's are the East and the West. And thus We have made you a middle people, that you might be witnesses to the people, and the Prophet a witness to you"* (2:143).

We see that the scope of Islam's confrontation and opposition to other ideologies, especially those that are concerned with the question of man, is as far-reaching as the very range and depth of its summons.

MYSTICISM, EQUALITY, AND FREEDOM

I SHOULD LIKE TO PROPOSE that we, in effect, step out of our sectarian limitations and explore the world in which we now live, and the nature and the humanity that dwell in that world. Nature and humanity are two very basic subjects; there is no doubt about that. In order to explore these two subjects and their interrelation, and to explore the life and movement of man, we should consider all the intellectual schools and experiences that in the course of history have come forward as religion, philosophy, or various other fields of human thought and action. In correlating all these, we arrive at three basic currents; all other matters prove to be either branches of these three or else altogether unrelated and secondary questions. These three basic currents, then, are mysticism, equality, and freedom.

Mysticism, in its most general sense, has always existed in both the East and the West. The reason it is spoken of as having arisen in the East, and has acquired an Eastern mien, is not that only the Oriental has an aptitude for mysticism, but rather that, because civilization first arose in the East, the birthplace of thought, culture, and the great religions, mysticism must also, as a matter of course, have had its beginnings there. In the savage environment of the Western hemisphere, mankind had not yet reached civilization; naturally it could not have possessed this sublime mysticism. But in general, mysticism is innate to human nature.

It even seems to me that Darwin, who is attacked as being such a materialist, goes further than anyone in affirming the reality of human spirituality. In scientific language, Darwin says, "Evolution assumed a material, physiological, and bodily form in non-human life-forms, in plants and animals: plant life found diffusion; then the amoeba and other forms of animal life came into existence, each species being transformed into another more highly evolved one. Then the proto-man, the most evolved of animals, evolved still further; for instance, the hair fell from his palms and his forehead broadened, his chin receded, and his tail disappeared; he stood erect: man had come into being." From this point onward, however, the process of human evolution was not physical, but on the inner, spiritual level.

What occasioned this parting of ways for man and his animal forebears, the ape-men, and launched man on his properly human course was the appearance of the mystical sense. Thus, this first man—whether of the East or the West—has this sense, which, we must note, is a rudimentary one, not of intellectual or scientific value. What this man feels toward some rocks or toward an idol, the numinous quality he senses in certain things, the mysterious tie with them he feels in his being, is the source of his mystical sense and disposition. However, since this is such a primitive stage of humanity, these symbols are valueless. What gave Eastern mysticism such depth and grandeur was the height to which Eastern civilization and culture had risen.

The progress of a given religion is bound up with the progress that its followers achieve. We can readily appreciate this. We see how the Hindus—until about a century ago— were regarded by the Muslims as the very epitome of backwardness, decadence, shirk, and ignorance, with their cow worship and all that. Now we are virtually overrun with books about Hinduism, and the books written about Islam cannot be compared to them. Radhakrishnan has written a philosophical interpretation of the sanctity of the cow with which none of our books about tauhid can compare. Hindu intellectuals are now offering interpretations of shirk and the countless gods of India that rank with the world's most sublime philosophical thought. Meanwhile, we have a highly advanced religion (at least from a historical standpoint, two thousand years more evolved than that of the Hindus),which, in our hands, has become something banal and commonplace. At any rate, mysticism is an intellectual current arising from the essential nature of man. The most general meaning of the word "mysticism" is the inner sense of apprehension people have while here in the world of nature, so that whoever is lacking this sense of apprehension has clearly not yet arrived at the specifically human stage. He has merely lost his tail and shed some hair. Otherwise, it is impossible in our earthly, material life, in relation to this sky and this natural order, for people not to feel agitated.

This sense of agitation arises because of some deficiency in man's relation to nature. That is to say, man *qua* man experiences needs that nature can no longer satisfy. Why not? Because nature is a home in which man and cow, animal and plant, live together; it is constructed according to the needs of the animal. Man who has come into being in this world of nature has needs that nature, the home he shares with the animals, cannot fulfill. That is what produces a lack, a sense of alienation and exile in us while we are in this world. Thus we feel a thirst and a sense of estrangement, which are the wellsprings of the mystical spirit within us. Therefore, it is only natural that, in order to fulfill this need, this thirst, we should ponder over what is lacking in this world. It is natural that we should look beyond nature to satisfy needs that are supra-material, and that we should journey to those places where the things needed are to be found. The more we outgrow nature, the more alien to it we become, and the stronger our sense of exile and loneliness grows. To relieve this loneliness and to flee this exile, we look to a world that is not here.

In a word, the world not here is the "unseen." Thus, we may succinctly say that mysticism is a manifestation of the primordial nature of man and it exists as a means of journeying to the unseen. But where is this unseen? In attempting to answer this question, we tend to fall into the lap of some particular sect again, some mystical or Sufi school, and that I intend to avoid. I will say that what we all hold in common is our belonging to a species that in principle seeks the unseen, and that is the source of its behavior and its development. If what man sees and feels were enough, he would remain static, but since it is not enough, he goes into motion, a motion that ensures his evolution.

If this mystical sense were taken away from man, he would at once revert to being a very highly developed, intelligent, and strong animal, dominating nature, successfully providing for his needs—whereas man is more than that. It is the mystical sense that endows man with excellence and nobility; the more highly developed a person is, the stronger this need, this thirst, becomes. As we may judge for ourselves, those who are more highly developed are more dissatisfied. Those whose spiritual development is greater have more sublime needs and skills that are less physical, and nature is less able to satisfy them. That much is clear. It is clear even when we consider materialists who have evolved but who do not believe in God or the unseen, such as Dostoevsky (who, in a sense, is religious), Sartre (who is not at all religious and is opposed to the idea of God and the unseen), and Albert Camus (who is beyond any doubt a materialist). We see that they are materialists from an intellectual standpoint, but not in spirit, because their thoughts and feelings toward the spirit are highly developed, and they regret the non-existence of God.

Thus, contrary to what the materialists say—that man's propensity for the unseen degrades him—we might say that man's propensity for what actually exists degrades him. By pursuing values that do not exist in nature, he is lifted above nature, and the spiritual and essential development of the species is secured. Mysticism is thus a lantern shining within humanity. It is a catalyst that transforms material man into a non-material entity above and beyond the limits of nature. It is a line drawing him to what is not here. That constitutes his spiritual evolution. Regardless of their ordinances relating to daily life, economics, politics, morals, and the like, all the religions have this single root of mysticism. Being Eastern or Western, monotheistic or polytheistic, cannot change this, for these matters relate only to the type of religion and its degree of evolution.

This is very interesting: Sartre no longer says (as a nineteenth-century thinker might have) that there is no God and religion is a superstition that afflicts people. He says instead that God's non-existence has made all existence idiotic and pointless, but that's the way it is; what can we do about it? With God removed from nature, Sartre plainly feels it as constricting, idiotic, unfeeling, inadequate to human needs. He affirms the fact of human exile and alienation in nature, only he does not believe in God. He also maintains that with God out of the way, anything is permissible, since only God's existence makes good and evil credible.

Without God, it is as if there were a house in which there is no one, no eye to see. About being in such a house, one does not ask: How am I to sit? How am I to dress? How am I to act? Such questions are meaningless. To sit in a mannerly or an unmannerly way in a house in which there is no eye to observe you makes no real difference. To differentiate sitting properly from sitting improperly, to distinguish beauty from ugliness, good behavior from bad, fair speech from foul, requires the existence of an observer. If there is no seeing eye in nature to supervise, there is no difference between the treacherous and the faithful, or between the person who sacrifices himself to faith and values and the one who sacrifices others to his self-aggrandizement. They are all alike in that there is no absolute standard external to their actions.

All this goes to show the way these thinkers perceive the absence of God and religion as a lack; however, by failing to believe in them, such thinkers only reinforce this lack, as well as our loneliness, our being condemned to exile. This shows how the primordial nature of man outgrows the potentials of the natural world. If people lack this mystical apprehension, they freeze or wither spiritually. We see this in the way today's civilization has evolved without God, taking the form of a civilized society of savage people. Today, a science developed without God has actually produced a civilized society, but not civilized people, whereas in the past, we had civilized people in a savage and backward society.

Mysticism carries human cultural and spiritual growth to the absolute pinnacle, to God. It is one of the three basic intellectual currents. Eastern mysticism, however, was later to enter religion, which gradually assumed the form of an ecclesiastical establishment and gave rise to a new class. As part of the ruling class, it formed social ties with the other elements of that class. The unfortunate consequence was that religion and mysticism were transformed into a superstitious rationale for the exploitation of the people by the ruling class and into an enemy of human growth, the growth of man's primordial nature. Mysticism became a shackle on the foot of the spiritual and material evolution of mankind. Those spirits who sought freedom necessarily found themselves opposing such a religion; they had no alternative.

WE DO NOT ASK that European liberalism deduce the essential truth of Islam from the Qur'an or the essential truth of Christianity from history, since when the religious classes themselves fail to infer the truth, how can we expect some European writer, socialist, or worker to do so? And so it happened that the next major movement, in its pursuit of human freedom and scientific and intellectual growth, came to oppose religion as a matter of course. Likewise, religion, fallen into the paralytic hands of the custodians of the Middle Ages, and thus assuming a reactionary and inhuman role, opposed this new movement and therefore automatically followed the fateful course we have described, first in Europe, and, in time, throughout the world. Thus it was universally said: Human liberation entirely depends on the removal of the fetters that religion placed on people's hands and feet. Of course, by fetters, I mean the constraints that the religious establishment in Islam and Christianity, as well as in Judaism, Hinduism, and all the faiths, have imposed on human thought.

This new trend in Europe essentially began by coalescing around questions of equality, justice, and humanism—matters that are always among our human thoughts and ideals. But then, in the nineteenth century, the advent of the machine intensified class contradictions, oppression, and the gap between the rich and the poor. The new situation differed greatly from the earlier one, when a landowner might have employed twenty or thirty peasants. How much could a single peasant produce in a year? Suppose he produced five *kharvars*[1] of wheat. One would go for seed and initial expenses, one was spent in procuring land and water, and one would be for the peasant's own use. So, to what extent could the landlord exploit the peasant? He couldn't appropriate anything more than two-fifths of the crop. Why is that? Because the peasant could not possibly produce any more. In the past, therefore, exploitation always occurred at a fixed and low level.

If someone wanted to exploit on a larger scale, he had to recruit the services of more individuals; that is, since he could not increase productivity, he had to enlarge the labor force. For instance, to appropriate two thousand *kharvars* of wheat would require recruiting one thousand peasants. Now that was impossible. No one could import all the labor he wished; sufficient land and water were not available. Production levels, therefore, remained perpetually static. Well, production might rise fifty maunds[2] in a rainy year or decline one hundred in a dry one, but it remained the same overall.

In the eighteenth and nineteenth centuries, however, the machine entered the picture and increased production a hundredfold. That is, the peasant, now a worker standing alongside a machine, could work ten, twenty, one hundred times faster. Five shoemakers working for one employer could make ten to fifteen pairs of shoes a day, but working with a machine they could produce a thousand pairs, which is to say, production had increased a hundredfold, while nowhere did workmen's wages increase a hundredfold. Suppose they doubled or tripled; the rest would go to the employer, who formerly took only two-fifths of the yield.

[1] One *kharvar* = 300 kilograms. (TR.)

[2] One maund = about 3 kilograms. (TR.)

This exploitation has resulted in greater accumulations of wealth alongside more stark poverty. A peasant formerly could keep several cows, sheep, and chickens at his home to live on. He had his own small plot of land. Likewise, most implements of production, such as a mule, pick and shovel, belonged to the peasant. Thus the peasant was himself a sort of proprietor. When he became a worker, however, as he left home in the morning, he had nothing to take with him but his workclothes and a clean shave. He simply took his good right arm to the factory for eight hours and tired himself out, to collect, say twenty *tumans*[3] and go home. Not being able to afford a moment's negligence, he would become daily more wedded to the machine. The peasant, on the other hand, had been a free man, working for five months out of the year and deciding himself what was to be done. He felt free. But for the worker, this sense of freedom no longer exists, nor is there a moment's leisure to think, a moment's escape from work.

And so it went, until class differences reached their greatest and grew still worse. The capital that in former times had been scattered among thousands of shops, businesses, and the like, became concentrated in the hands of five or ten, or perhaps twenty individuals; the others were systematically disarmed and transformed into huge masses of workers.

Now it was that the perpetual search of people and religions for justice and equality took a disastrous and inhuman turn. People, societies, and nations came to be drawn into two terrible, mutually hostile camps, which were at each other's throats. But the true cause of the dispute was unclear. Spiritual values were banished and the free human conscience reacted spontaneously by rising in revolt against the situation. Thus the struggles engulfed first Europe, then Asia and Africa, and today this awareness is even stronger in Asia, Africa, and Latin America than in Europe, where it originated. Various schools have appeared for the purpose of resisting the capitalist system with its terrible exploitation of human beings, where the worker is deformed by the machine into a machine that must

---

[3] $2.63, at the current rate of exchange. Today one tuman = about $.13. (TR.)

run until it falls apart and is discarded, where there is no chance for human spiritual growth and the capitalist himself is converted into a sort of pack rat, feeling nothing but the urge to accumulate.

This struggle has emerged under various names around the world, but unfortunately, this tendency and movement, a popular movement for class justice and equitable social relations in the world, grew up in opposition to religion. That is because religion itself was controlled by the ruling class and a clerical class that had essentially grown up within the ruling order.

The religions at the time of their appearance had had no ruling class elements. This is especially true of Islam. And only today, I was reading a discussion of the same point in one of the writings of a group of Latin American revolutionaries. They are very proud of the fact that they can say, "We don't have producers and intellectuals; we are not divided into revolutionaries who act and intellectuals who think and construct an ideology, so we are all one. The same person who spreads the ideology acts, and the same person who acts also thinks. We are all one." It is clear that this question has also been resolved in Islam. Among the companions of the Prophet and the *mujahidin* in the early days of Islam, who is the intellectual, who the activist, who the cleric? Absolutely no such classifications exist. Everyone promulgates Islam, fights, and also farms, cultivates dates, or herds camels. That is, each person is simultaneously worker, warrior, and intellectual.

It is only later that classes appear and the clergy comes to comprise one of them. Since this official class must generally work to serve its class interests and help its class affiliates, it grafts those concerns onto the formal religion. It comes to narcotize the people. Thus official religion comes to oppose automatically the movement we have been discussing. It would fight this movement in Europe to its last breath, and continues to do so. Wherever it has arisen, in Latin America and elsewhere, the official religions have opposed it, solely in the name of religion.

This, then, is how modern thought perceives the issue: religion is essentially a rationale for the existing order, to the detriment of the people and the advantage of a minority; we see that is how things are in practice. There is another movement that has nothing at all to do with religion but only seeks to free some people from exploitation; religion charges that this movement has no faith at all. Clearly, there is nothing really religious about the question. Any talk of mysticism and spirituality here is a lie, but one that nevertheless serves to reinforce the status quo.

And so it is unfortunate that, in Europe, this movement, which certainly espouses individual and class equality and justice (that is to say, ideals that are fundamental to religion), emerged as an anti-religious force. It appeared as the socialist movement in its various forms: Marxist, anti-Marxist, syndicalist, and others, beginning in Europe and spreading across the world.

After this movement, there arose a third major movement, which found its greatest growth after World War II.[4]

MYSTICISM WAS SUBSUMED by religion, and religion, in turn, ceased to play a part in the lives of Europeans, so that only the priests and their followers remained within its sphere (and their time too is rapidly passing). As religion waned as a presence in the intellectual lives of the young, socialism took its place. But the goals of the nineteenth-century European socialists never reached fruition. We saw a socialist revolution in the Europe of a hundred years ago: the workers were revolutionary and capitalism was being swept aside. Now, however, a hundred years later, the workers of Europe are no longer like that. Especially in Germany—where the workers' movement was once at its most advanced, it is now at its most retarded. This is true to such a degree that the German working

---

[4] We speak of something as a "movement" when it becomes widespread. Before this point, the roots of these movements always existed in history, as thoughts and as schools. They come to be spoken of as movements when they become universal bases of action.

class is more rightist than even the Catholic and Protestant churches there. In all the thirty years since the War, there has not been one strike in Germany, whereas in the one hundred years before that, the workers were under the intellectual leadership, first, of Proudhon, then of Marx. At any rate, European capitalism was able to abort the socialist revolution completely. Socialism in other countries such as China and the Soviet Union has now come to a dead end.

This means the goals of the freedom-seeking people of the nineteeth century have not been realized. Those people felt that if a socialist system were realized in society, humanity would be freed from the bonds of materialism, and class differences and conflicting interests would cease to exist. They felt that without those contradictions, there would be no war, and without war and exploitation, all of the powers of humanity would be united and placed at the service of human development and spiritual growth. Although these were the goals of the nineteenth-century socialists, we have seen how that very socialist system that was to have freed people, as it was put into practice, wound up enslaving all to a single leader, and assumed the forms, first, of worship of personality and party, and then of worship of the state. Proudhon wrote in his letters to Marx:

> But if we want to carry anything out, it should be something very modest; we should carry it out only for the sake of people's awareness. We must not play the prophet again and impose ourselves on the people by placing a set of commands and proscriptions over them. We must not establish a new religion, a new cult in the world .... I am afraid that tomorrow this school of yours will assume the form of a state religion, and that worship of the state will replace worship of God.

We have seen it come out just as he foretold.

Disillusionment with this state of affairs has been reflected in the thought of free spirits, who have founded a new school denying, as they themselves say, both religion, which draws man into servitude to a god or gods, and Marxism, which enslaves man to the state.

When all wealth is in the hands of the state, and the state is set up as a hierarchy, it becomes established and evolves into a bureaucracy; the state thus takes the form of a self-perpetuating ruling clique. In such a system, no one will be able to do anything; no one will be able to rescue himself, because sufficient wealth and financial opportunity will not exist. All persons will be employees dependent upon this frightful organization capped with its leader.

It is strange that the very movement whose most basic premise is denial of the personality in history (it maintains that personality has no role in history) should emerge as the major breeding ground of personality. Its various divisions are even named after individuals: Marxism, Leninism, Titoism, Castroism, Trotskyism, Maoism, and many others that have disappeared. But should we, as followers of a religion, speak to someone of Muhammadism, or of a Muhammadist, or an Alyist, he wouldn't understand at all what we were talking about, since we, the religious (although we are accused of worshipping the Prophet, whom we believe to be the best of men), do not suffer from this personality complex. These people, however, are denying personality and maintaining that the individual, the hero, has not the slightest place in human life and history, while their schools take the form of leader-worship. It is another form of fascism.

World War II accomplished some very basic things. The first was to set religion before the world again as a serious force. The second was that it brought the pretentions of science into question. The third was that it dispelled some of the glamour of Marxism, since Marxism was unable to respond to the human and economic problems that arose. It was at this point that existentialism rose to prominence.

Existentialism, of course, had existed in the nineteenth century and even earlier—it exists in our own mysticism (in that mysticism is basically an existentialist philosophy)—but not in this new form in which it is now expounded in the world, which is centered on man. This form maintains that all through history, we have been speaking of something other than man—of the primacy of God, Who wishes to make men merely His followers.[5]

So existentialism returns to a reliance on human existence itself. It says to man, "Look carefully and see what there is; turn to yourself and look."[6] Why? Because he is always looking to something outside himself: to gods, to good and evil spirits. And now, even in the existing system, as he has let go of religion, his gaze becomes fixed upon material life, so that he spends all his time pursuing this thing, then that thing. He has stepped out of his own self and is pursuing matters external to himself. He searches for things he can rely upon. What has

[5] This refers, of course, to the relationship between man and God that appears in Christianity and the other religions, which actually distorts man into something other than himself. In [the present state of practice of] our own religion, a man who prays before God so corroborates mankind's abjectness and his own, that the poor fellow even ends up asking God and the Imam to pay off his debts, or to straighten out the traffic problem, just as if he himself didn't even exist or have a will of his own. He sees himself as having nothing, but it is not the "nothing" of philosophy, as when Islam speaks of humanity as having "nothing before God." This does not mean that man actually has nothing; rather it means that he has everything, and this "everything" is from God. The idea of spiritual poverty that exists in Islam means that man does not attribute his actual values to himself, lest he be overcome by pride. It does not mean that I have nothing, but rather that I have everything, as reflected in will, scientific knowledge, insight, and responsibility, and that I should employ all these for the good of my life. However, from a philosophical standpoint, I must attribute these to the power of God. I must not deny them. Our present-day religion denies the values and noble qualities of humanity that the Qur'an affirms. It says we have nothing to resort to but saints, intercessors, and tears. The religious outlook around the world is much the same.

[6] In verse 105 of the Surah al-Ma'idah [i.e., 10:105], God addresses the believers: "O ye who believe! Guard your own souls: if you follow (right) guidance, no hurt can come to you from those who stray. The goal of you all is to God: it is He that will show you the truth of all that ye do."
Islam restores man to himself; it maintains that whatever man may have, it comes from himself and is nothing but the result of his own efforts and strivings. Each one will soon see the results of his own strivings. A day (Resurrection) is approaching when each one will remember what he strived, struggled, and expended his powers to obtain, and will receive his reward: "Man shall have nothing but what he has strived for, and that which he strived for will be seen" (53:39-40). "The Day man will recall what he strove for" (79:35). (MOHAMMAD TAQI SHARI'ATI)

been forgotten here is the person himself, this "I" as a being. I don't give that a thought; I don't notice that my own existential values are being deformed, impaired, and eclipsed. Thus, existentialism is another way of restoring human existence to its primacy.

So we have arrived at our three basic currents.

The first current is the spiritual current, which relates humanity to being: mysticism, which sets forth this great tie as a world-view based on man.

The second current appears in socialism, in communism, in all the schools that speak of human equality and the abolition of class contradictions. These consider only the question of ordering the class relations of the two groups, the two poles, in the context of a single society: the ordering of the relations of landlord and peasant, of capitalist and worker, and of their social relations. By contrast, mysticism addresses the relations of world, man, and being.

The third current shows itself in existentialism, which maintains that the two other systems of relations forget man, or become caught up in an external question: in the case of socialism, with justice, capital, political and class warfare; in the case of mysticism, with the unseen, spirituality, and the like. Both have abandoned man.

So, it is time to turn back to humanity, say the existentialists. "Let us cleave to what both religion and socialism are trying to take away from us. Let us cling to our human freedom. I have freedom and choice. But socialism has seized all the initiative and handed it over to the state. It makes my decisions for me. It creates programs for me, determines my production and consumption, and eclipses me in an organizational hierarchy. Thus it takes away my freedom. Religion, too, looks to God for all that it seeks, and God is an entity external to the human essence; so religion negates human freedom.[7] Let us turn back to humanity itself; let us say, 'You exist. You are in

---

[7] God, just as he has given man freedom, has established limits and conditions upon that freedom, so that the consequences of his acts return only to himself, not to others. Hazrat Ali proclaims, "Where man chooses for his soul, if he safeguards it, it ascends, and if he degrades it, it is degraded." This is the

this world of nature an alien to nature. And no god exists, nor any tie. Therefore, cling to your own essential values, which are part of your specific essence; let them grow and evolve. Quiet your existential apprehension; look to it and answer it. You are nothing more than a thing among things, whence all your values originate. Choice and freedom are yours unconditionally. All values exist when this freedom exists; should this freedom be taken away from you, these values would cease to be; you would become as a slave to other powers: God or the state.' "

Now let us view these three currents from another standpoint. Let us examine their weak points.

The weak point of present-day extablished religion is this: it actually separates man from his own humanity. It makes him into an importunate beggar, a slave to unseen forces beyond his power; it deposes him and alienates him from his own will. It is this established religion that we are familiar with today.

This is socialism's weak point: it has been linked with materialism, and in practice it has turned out to mean state primacy and worship of the state, which in turn have become primacy of the head of state, the leader. Now, even if this leader is a witless functionary like Stalin, the people must acquire all their philosophical notions concerning socialism, which is a scientific discipline, from their esteemed leader! Whatever he has written has the force of revelation.

This is the weak point of existentialism: however much it may turn on the primacy of man and on human freedom, because it denies both God and social issues, it leaves man suspended in midair. When I am free to choose anything, because there is no other criterion, the question arises: On what basis am I to choose the good and reject the evil? Existentialism lacks a basis on which to answer my question. Now I am bent

---

best proof that, while man has absolute freedom (choice), the results of his actions are entirely able to effect either his progress or his debasement. It is clear that the religion to which the text refers is a stiff and formal one, not the actual religion of Islam. (MOHAMMAD TAQI SHARI'ATI)

on a course of action where I may either sacrifice myself to the people or sacrifice the people to myself, and I am free; which am I to choose? Existentialism does not say which to choose, since there is no rational grounds for it to do so because it is neither socialistic nor theistic. Consequently, it leaves people free; they end up just like the European existentialists, personally free to indulge in whatever dirty business they care to. That is because individual freedom without a specified direction will be debased and reduced to a veritable cesspool of corruption and filth; it is certain to result in the pollution of freedom.

But as for the positive sides of the three major currents: if mysticism did not exist, if man lacked that sense of apprehension, we would essentially have no man. Speech, thought, and consciousness are not the real signs of humanity. Today it has been proven that what was once said, that animals function through instinct while only man functions through intellect, is nonsense. Today we can observe animals reasoning from premises to conclusions with an intelligence that Socrates and Plato could not approach; they are able to produce a fresh and creative response to a given event in a way that cannot be described as instinctual. The same might be said of speech. In my opinion, what distinguishes man from all the animals is his sense of apprehension before the unseen, in other words, the inadequacy of nature to fulfill his needs and his existence, and his consequent flight from what is toward what ought to be—not toward what is or isn't, but *what ought to be*. Here is the proof of the sublime and spiritual in man.

Love is a power, a heat that is not produced by the calories or proteins I ingest. It has an unknowable source and can inflame and melt all of my existence; it even impels me to self-denial. Love grants me values higher and more sublime than expediency; and no physical, material, or biochemical account can comprehend it. If love were taken away from man, he would become an isolated, stagnant being, useful only to the systems of production. He might become an engineer or doctor, but that *quality of being a man*, that extra-material energy— through which men have made history and have forged the great revolutions—would die within his nature, and that burning would cease.

I DISCUSSED A QUESTION at the Husayniya-yi Irshad, and then put it to the students. Several gave answers. I said, "No!" I wanted to create a struggle in their intellects, so I didn't give an answer. A brother from the provinces objected. Someone stood up to demand that I immediately give an answer to put everyone at ease. I said, "Dear sir, I have come to disturb the comfortable. Did you imagine I was opium or heroin, to make everyone feel easy? I am not one of those who have the answers all written out."

If someone really wants to perform a service, he should make comfortable people uncomfortable, and calm people agitated. He should plant contradiction and conflict in stagnant people. By God, it would be a thousand times over a greater service to sow doubt among some of these people than to sow certainty, since that certainty is being injected into people at such a rate that it acts like a narcotic; it is worthless. We 700 million Muslims have a certainty that is not worth two bits. What comes into existence after doubt, anxiety, and agitation has value: "Belief after unbelief!"

Yes, certainty arrived at after unbelief and the exercise of choice has value. We see the other kind of certainty all through history, and it is worthless. The verse *"The people were a single nation"* (2:213) attacks the possessors of certainty. The prophets came essentially to produce controversy. Otherwise, the people would have gone right on grazing peacefully in their folly.

WE SHOULD BEGIN to summarize, as much as possible; so the three fundamental intellectual and spiritual currents (giving primacy to existence, justice, and love), and in particular, mysticism, must be more clearly distinguished. Mysticism follows love. Love is the extra-material energy that is the source and active cause of human behavior. The next current is based on equality and material justice among people, and the third represents freedom and choice for man.

I think, then, that we should sum up these three basic currents (all other human currents are either branches of these three, or trivial) in three words: one is love, which lies at the origin of the mystical schools; religion is also a manifestation of it. The second is material justice among classes and nations, as it applies to colonization and domestic exploitation. The third is the primacy of human existence, which implies the need to return to, and rely upon, the essential and specific core of human values; to grant freedom and choice to the human "I" itself, for its growth and perfection; to open our eyes to the essence of man; and to promote the existential "I," which is being lost within the capitalist system, is expressly denied by the religious system, and becomes one-dimensional within socialism.

To make matters clearer, I think we should take the individual as an example. Each of these currents is a factor in both human development and human aberration. That is, insofar as they concentrate on one direction but neglect the others, they each constitute a defective kind of guidance.

Mysticism produces a spiritual sensitivity in man, along with sublime psychological and spiritual values, which foster his existence and his spirit. However, it blinds him to and makes him heedless of some of the disastrous conditions around him. In fact, this is exactly the case of the man who, in a state of spiritual seclusion, ascends in spirit to the sky, to the "lotus tree of the ends of the earth." Outside the wall of his place of retreat oppression, disaster, poverty, shameful acts, ignorance, corruption, and decadence are dishonoring all the spiritual values of man, but he never becomes aware of it; that is, his connection with the reality of his environment has been completely severed. That is how this mode of human deliverance is transformed into a kind of egotism; each is searching for a way to go to paradise alone. But how is such a person fit for paradise who is harder of heart than a corrupt and materialistic person, than even an animal, which feels an instinctive sympathy toward others? It is true that he is following the path of worship, devotion, and religious exercises, which leads to God and paradise, but even so, he is an egotist. Even if he does attain paradise, he is an egotist, and the egotist is something less than an animal. Paradise has animals as well. Getting to paradise is not important; to be human and reach paradise is important.

I have always felt nothing but the deepest faith in and devotion to men like Shams-e Tabrizi and Moulavi [Rumi]. As we stand before them, it is as if we stand before a sun, such is their greatness. As we look upon Moulavi, it is as if he stands at the forefront of all the human beings that we know anything about, in the aspects of spiritual growth and personal character. But for the society of Balkh or of Konya, for the Islamic society of his day, his presence or absence made no difference. For he was, to some extent, held confined by a spiritual and divine quarantine, which permitted him to feel nothing of the circumstances around him—the oppression, the Mongol wars, the Crusades. Somewhat similar is the case of the French poet Gautier who once in wartime stated, "I prefer lying down to sitting, I prefer sitting to standing, and I prefer remaining home to going out. I will know nothing of the war they say has engulfed the whole world, unless a bullet shatters the window of my house." At any rate, how is it possible that, on the one hand, a man should find spiritual growth, and, on the other, he should be so indifferent to such a plain and simple spiritual truth?

The person who judges in a one-dimensional way will regard mysticism as stemming from a senseless and stupefying superstition, but it is our practice to examine all the dimensions of a given question. From one standpoint, we see that mysticism has created a sublime tie: in no other school is man so exalted as in mysticism. Our mystical schools have given us men the like of whom we see in no other school, in no revolution. Great revolutions have produced great heroes, but their human personalities do not bear comparison with the personalities of our mystical tradition. They do not deserve to be mentioned in the same breath. To deny the selfish urges, weaknesses, and private daydreams that dwell in each of us, to combat virtually all the powers that go to make up our nature, and to bring to fruition the root of love and mysticism, the fire in man's existence and essence: these are no trifling accomplishments. Nevertheless, we see that they produce a negative and empty sort of person, the greatest boon to executioners, to agents of oppression, reaction, colonialism, and the like. The tyrants of history have always been indebted to such people because they never stick their noses into other people's business.

The case with socialism is much the same: we see a youth whose very being socialism, whether materialistic or not (but generally so), has enveloped head to foot. This youth is totally bent on seeing that an employer does not embezzle five *tumans* of the worker's thirty-*tuman* wage, and if he has embezzled it, the youth is ready to part with his life, soul, being, and love in order to see that the worker, or some peasant, someone who has suffered oppression, is awarded his due. When we consider this youth as a human being, however, we see that he thinks solely about questions of socialism, of the economic relations between two classes. Because of his narrow, one-sided attention to this class relationship within society, he has become walled in by this one particular subject; all existential and human dimensions, values, and needs are completely lost on him. Is this right? Whenever I see some acquaintance, friend, or student so anxious and upset about the question of class exploitation that he comes to see all the questions of the world only through this peep-hole and thinks of nothing else day and night, I feel sorry for him, for he is so very eager to sacrifice himself, and he shows such a strong aptitude and spiritual leaning.[8] He has sacrificed his whole life to one idea. Why should he be deprived of all the experiences that are available in culture, history, religion, or just in life, and that are conducive to the growth of man's other dimen-

---

[8] That is because this is a purely material matter for the worker, but for the youth, to whose life and soul it imparts spiritual meaning, it is a spiritual question.

sions? Why should he think of nothing but this one question? He ends up a person who is more moved by a simple newspaper quotation of some politician than by the whole of [Rumi's] *Masnavi.* All that has been spoken, all the spiritual values in human history, mean nothing to him; all the examples of moral growth in particular people are unknown to him. Anyone whom this youth believes to be not a socialist—even though he may be heroic, self-sacrificing, and anti-colonialist, though he achieves the utmost in courage from a moral standpoint, sacrificing his whole material life for the sake of his conviction—isn't worth a cent to him. He cannot understand the merits of such a person at all.

We see that socialism removes from man all his limbs and branches except one, but it so encourages that one to spread out that it outgrows root and trunk. Thus, it makes man onedimensional, however lofty and sublime that one dimension may be. It really is not so different from the case of mysticism. They are both tiny peep-holes, with the difference that one opens onto a social sensibility, and the other, onto a universal and existential sensibility.

Now, we see, man is alienated from himself and unwitting if he worships heaven and the unseen, belongs to a socialist school, or lives under a dictatorship. And in terms of the economic system, he has been alienated and dazzled by money; it is as if money had swallowed him whole: he is so alienated by consumption and pleasurable pursuits that he no longer exists. Insofar as pleasure and consumption have taken hold of him, he is nothing, and the remainder of him is a cipher.

This man, whom the machine, capitalism, dictatorships, administrative bureaucracies, and the materialistic life of consumption have alienated from himself, is today taking back his own existential primacy, and that is the greatest service existentialism has done man. Existentialism has revived the issues of the primacy of existence, of human freedom, of growth of the inner man, of the sublime "I" of man. It centers itself on these things and increases people's awareness of them. This constitutes a kind of return to the human self-awareness that was totally lost for centuries. Thus, it is a kind of deliverance, or a call to deliverance, from these systems, these intellectual and material bonds. However, speaking in terms of spirit, it does have this other side: Now that I am free, what am I to do? It has no answer to this question. Two steps are at issue here: whoever wishes to take my hand and provide me with the means to escape this prison should have an object in mind and a program after I escape; otherwise, I will have nothing to do. My freedom might turn into vagrancy, in which case it would no longer be clear that I was well served in being set free. If freedom has no purpose and touchstone, it is vagrancy; next it will turn into futility, and after that it will take the form of Western existentialism, whose goal is to go looking for hashish in Nepal or the Khyber Pass.

AT ANY RATE, these three essential currents, real and actual, exist in the depths of the human temperament and produce the most basic needs of human existence in the forms of three manifestations: one of them, love and mysticism; the second, the search for justice, as illustrated by the movements of the nineteenth and twentieth centuries[9]; and the third, existentialism, currently being pursued by European intellectuals. They exist as means of escape from the systems that deny man, and as means for a return to man.

Therefore, the most perfect person or school for the purpose of liberating man would be the person or school that embraces these essential dimensions. If all three dimensions existed in a single school, none of the negative dimensions of any school would have a place in it, since one dimension would compensate for the negative aspect of another dimension. When these three dimensions each separately take the form of schools, their negative aspects are actualized, whereas

---

[9] These spread across the outer layer of European society in the nineteenth century, and of Asian society in the twentieth, and then they engulfed African and Latin American societies, which had been sacrificed to the oppression and exploitation of multi-national capitalism.

if these three dimensions were united, their negative aspects could no longer exist. If a school made me more attentive to my social responsibility than a socialist, mysticism would no longer make me heedless of social responsibility. That is, if mysticism tends to render me devoid of social responsibility, or responsibility toward others, and to keep me occupied solely with my existential and spiritual development, that other dimension of my school, belief in equality, would not allow this to happen. In short, from one side, Sartre summons me to my own existential freedom; from another, socialism summons me to social responsibility; from yet another, mysticism and love summon me to the world of being and life, and to the final destiny of my existence and species, and they inflame me with a heat that arises from beyond social life and even from beyond my individual, existential self.

If I, then, living in the twentieth century, were to incorporate all three currents into a school, this school would secure for me a multi-dimensional, balanced, harmonious growth. In my opinion, we need look no further for an example than Islam. That is precisely its value—that it is harmoniously centered on all three dimensions. Its origin, spirit, and (as in the case of all religions, including Christianity) essence is mysticism. However, it emphasizes social justice and the fate of others, even of a single other, and it says, "If you keep one other person alive or revive him, it is as if you have revived all men, and if you kill another person, it is as if you have killed all other men."[10] That is, it is just that sensitive to my relation to others. Usury is a social and class problem, but Islam hates the usurer in a way that it does not hate the *mushrik* or the hypocrite.[11] Here, its particular emphasis is upon social issues, my relation with the society in which I live; it shows itself

---

[10] "On that account: We ordained for the Children of Israel that if any one slew a person—unless it be for murder or for spreading mischief in the land—it would be as if he slew the whole people: and if any one saved a life, it would be as if he saved the life of the whole people" (5:35). (MOHAMMAD TAQI SHARI'ATI)

[11] Concerning usury, God proclaims, "O ye who believe! Fear God, and give up what remains of your demand for usury, if ye are indeed believers. If ye do it not, take notice of war from God and His Apostle" (2:278-279). (MOHAMMAD TAQI SHARI'ATI)

sensitive to this question. In the case of the existential question Sartre speaks of, Islam takes a position altogether opposed to that of the established religions and even that of mysticism, which make man heedless of his own existence before God, which negate man before God's existence. Islamic *tauhid* is the only unitarian faith that affirms man's existence before God. There is no one who knows the God of Islam in full awareness, the way Islam itself has presented Him (not in the manner the inherited religious sensibility in Shi'ism and Sunnism, in fact everywhere, has brought about), and who has acquired his faith from Islam, who has not in consequence apprehended the sublimity of his own existence, his own kinship with God, while also experiencing the sublimity of his progressive development from the level of the higher animals to a divine rank. It is through the Islamic God of *tauhid* that man finds such greatness, growth, and perfection. Along with the actualization of love, He gives man greatness and nobility conjoined with humility. He dispenses these attributes to such a degree that man passes beyond the limits of existing beings.

This is not the mighty God Who affirms only Himself, of Whom Feuerbach says, "The poor have powerful gods; the poorer and more miserable they are, the stronger and more powerful are their gods." (That is the relationship that obtains in the mystical religions and in the present-day established religions.) On the contrary, to the extent that the man of *tauhid* perceives his poverty, he perceives his wealth; to the extent that he feels humility, he feels a pride, a glory, within himself; to the extent that he has surrendered to the service of God, he rises against whatever other powers, systems, and relations exist. Thus, in Islam, there actually exists a paradoxical relation between man and God—a simultaneous denial and affirmation, a becoming nothing and all, essentially an effacement and a transformation into a divine being during natural, material life.

Setting aside feelings of sectarian partisanship,[12] we maintain that Ali as he is known to us, all things considered, is

---

[12] Although I might be accused of the opposite, I don't think anyone would accuse me of this. [Some persons had accused Shari'ati of imperfect devotion to Shi'ism.]

the perfect exemplar and manifestation of the three basic dimensions.[13] As for love, that heavenly energy that draws man into a state of apprehension, burning, hunger and thirst within material life—it literally erupts from him. No other man is so inflamed with it as he is; it is so intense that sometimes it transports him out of himself, and he shouts in the desert. Of course, we in our unawareness imagine this stems from the anguish that was rained down upon him in Madinah, or was because of Fadak.[14] In fact, his very existence is aflame; he cries out like a volcano. Life and being are unbearable to him; love has hurled him from the face of the earth, out of time, toward the unseen. Then, another dimension brings him back to earth and makes him aware of the visible realities of politics and daily existence, so that he can show a degree of sensitivity to the fate of an orphan, or to that of a woman oppressed by the government of his state (a Jewish woman), that no socialist or responsible statesman has manifested. The pain it brings him reaches such intensity that he says, "Under my rule, a woman has been oppressed and transgressed against; if I die, do not reproach me, for the pain from this disgrace is enough to kill a man." Finally, from the existential standpoint, he is the best manifestation of man's existence; that is, he is a human being surpassing all others, and as the final outgrowth of the

---

[13] We find the following in the seventy-fourth "wisdom" of the *Nahj ul Balagah*, concerning the inward apprehension of Hazrat Ali (upon whom be peace) and his state of mental agitation, his being drowned in a sea of worship and attentiveness to God. Dirar ibn Hamzah Dabbabi, one of the companions most praised by the Imam (upon whom be peace), coming before Mu'awiyah and being asked by him concerning the well-being of Hazrat Ali, answered: "In some places where he was engaged in worship, and I was observing his states, as night spread its dark mantle, he stood at the *mihrab* of worship clutching his beard, writhing upon himself like one bitten by a snake, crying like one whom great sorrow had touched. He said concerning the world: 'O world! O world! Do you present yourself to me? Pass me by. Do you lean toward me in eagerness? May your deceit not be near; I have no need of you. Go deceive another; you are so far from me that I have triply divorced you, and there is no turning back. Your life is brief, your worth slight, and your desire base. Alas for the lack of provisions, the length of the road, the distance of the journey, and the demands of the appointed meeting!' " (MOHAMMAD TAQI SHARI'ATI)

[14] That is, due to the disputes over title to this village. (TR.)

visible, material, and inborn values of man (of this flesh-and-blood man, not of a spirit or archetype), he is the most perfect of men. He clearly places greater reliance upon human values and noble acts in his life and school than do any others. If we actually regard this school of Ali from the standpoint of the three major dimensions, the primacies of existence, justice, and mysticism (the inner light of the human essence), I believe we will satisfy the needs of our own time in the best way possible. As our children become socialists, their mystical sense and spirituality are lost. As they become mystics, they grow so indifferent to social problems that their very mysticism inspires loathing. As they leave both of these behind, and arrive at that existential "I" and existentialist freedom, they turn into hippies, Western existentialists and worthless denizens of cafes.

Now then, these three dimensions represent needs existing in the essence of our humanity and in our age. I believe that if we devote ourselves exclusively to any one of them, we will fall into a well, and remain negligent of the other two human dimensions. A conscious and balanced reliance on the school I have proposed implies more than just the discovery of Islam and a worshipful reverence for inner truth. Rather, if we draw from all three of the streams issuing from the one spring in order to satisfy the needs of today's man, and if we regard Islam from these three points of view, we will readily act according to our social responsibility.

R. Campbell, the translator, is currently doing graduate work in the Near Eastern Studies Department at the University of California, Berkeley. His work for Mizan Press also includes the translation of an anthology of writings by Ayatullah Taleghani.

Hamid Algar, the series editor for the books in this Contemporary Islamic Thought—Persian Series, is Professor of Persian and Islamic Studies in the Department of Near Eastern Studies at the University of California, Berkeley, where he has taught since 1965.

ALSO PUBLISHED BY
MIZAN PRESS

ON THE SOCIOLOGY OF ISLAM: Lectures
Ali Shari'ati
Translated by Hamid Algar

An anthology presenting some of the dynamic teacher's major ideas and introducing his coherent and contemporary Islamic world-view based on *tauhid.*

ISLAM AND REVOLUTION: Writings and Declarations of Imam Khomeini
Translated and annotated by Hamid Algar

The first complete English translation from the Persian of Khomeini's principal work on the political principles of Islam. Also, the text of some of his lectures, speeches, messages to the Iranian people, and interviews with the translator. With an introduction by the translator.

SOCIETY AND ECONOMICS IN ISLAM
Ayatullah Sayyid Mahmud Taleghani
Translated by R. Campbell

Includes short works on the subjects of *jihad* and economics by the recently deceased Ayatullah Taleghani (1910-1979). Also contains an excerpt from *A Ray From the Qur'an,* his well-known commentary and interpretation of the Qur'an.

MIZAN PRESS
P.O. Box 4065
Berkeley, California 94704